P9-BXW-208

YOUTH
SPECIALTIES

A

ACADEMIC

COMPANION
GUIDE

THIS WAY TO YOUTH MINISTRY

READINGS, CASE STUDIES,
RESOURCES TO BEGIN THE JOURNEY

DUFFY ROBBINS AND **LEN KAGELER**

YOUTH
SPECIALTIES

ACADEMIC

This Way to Youth Ministry Companion Guide
Copyright © 2004 by Youth Specialties

Youth Specialties Books, 300 South Pierce Street, El Cajon, CA 92020, are published by Zondervan,
5300 Patterson Avenue SE, Grand Rapids, MI 49530

Editorial and art direction by Rick Marschall
Editing by Laura Gross
Proofreading by Anita Palmer and Janie Wilkerson
Cover design by electricurrent
Interior design by Sarah Jongsma
Printed in the United States of America

04 05 06 07 08 09 / DC / 10 9 8 7 6 5 4 3 2 1

CONTENTS

UNIT 1: JOURNEY FROM THE INSIDE OUT

UNIT 2: UNDERSTANDING THE TERRAIN

UNIT 3: CHARTING A COURSE FOR THE JOURNEY

11045i

APPENDIXES

FORWARD!

At the heart of the gospel is this awesome truth: "The Word became flesh" (John 1:14). It's a statement that drew a line in the sand of human history, because it proclaimed the stunning fact that God came to this planet as a human being and lived in our midst. Not content to speak in general terms through his prophets, through his works, and through his words, God wanted to put flesh on his love. This was God incarnate—God with meat on his bones, God with sweat on his brow, God with sawdust on his robe, God with dirt on his sandals, and ultimately God with nails in his hands.

"The Word became flesh." It is this grand fact that must shape everything that we do in youth ministry. To reduce ministry to mere concepts, lessons, and theories—the Word became word?—without thinking seriously about how those concepts play out in the flesh and messiness and wonder of everyday youth ministry is to betray the message that moves us.

That, in a nutshell, is the idea that defines this Companion Guide you hold in your hands. This guide is an attempt to help you flesh out the ideas, concepts, and issues raised in your textbook, *This Way to Youth Ministry*. The reflection questions, the case studies, the writing projects, the suggestions for further study, and the appendix articles in the back of the book are all here for one reason: to help you connect the "Word became word" with the "Word became flesh."

In *This Way to Youth Ministry*, textbook and *Companion Guide* both, we employ metaphors of Journey and Exploration, of exciting trails ahead. There are two ways to approach every journey: one is to walk the trail, and the other is to explore the trail. Both approaches get you from point A to point B, but those who explore will get the full experience of the journey. Don't settle for explanation—the Word become textbook, so to speak—when the real adventure in the journey is through exploration—the Word become life!

Len Kageler has done a masterful job in this book of pulling together case studies, discussion ideas, and resources for further study. His years of front-line youth ministry experience spill out on every page, the overflow of one who knows what it's like to do ministry "in the trenches." His two-fisted grip on both youth ministry theory and practice make him a worthy guide in the adventure that lies ahead. If youth ministry is an adventure, then Len Kageler is the guy who will gather us around the campfire at the end of each chapter and tell us some stories about others who have walked the trail. Some of these stories warn us of potential dangers. Some of them alert us to sights we'll want to see. Some of them give us input about how to maximize the journey's enjoyment. But all of them are designed to make the sights and the sounds of the journey more vivid.

I hope you'll take full advantage of this resource. I'm excited that you are being provided with this gear for the journey. Walk carefully, listen fully, watch expectantly, read thoughtfully, discuss honestly, and reflect prayerfully. You have an exciting journey ahead. And now, this way to youth ministry...

A WORD TO STUDENTS

Welcome to the adventure! Thumbing through the main textbook to which this book is a Companion Guide, *This Way to Youth Ministry*, you're likely to be reminded that youth ministry is more than throwing frisbees, hangin' out, and eating cheeseburgers with kids. Duffy Robbins' text is great academics. I mean this in the most positive sense. His text puts you in touch with the major foundational concepts and theoretical bases that underpin the practice of youth ministry as it is done today.

The purpose of the companion text you now hold in your hand is twofold.

The first is to help you process, experience, and apply the concepts in *This Way to Youth Ministry*.

All of the case studies are real. Names have been changed; but there's nothing made up about them. I am grateful for the 15 church and parachurch youth workers who contributed case studies. I contributed the remainder. After two decades as a youth pastor and the last decade as a volunteer junior high youth worker, I've experienced some pretty crazy things—some wonderful and some terrible. You'll see.

You'll be asked to reflect on the cases in light of your own experience and the material in Robbins' text. You'll be asked to expand your understanding with some Internet-based assignments. You'll be asked to work collaboratively. You'll use TV and movie clips and be given the opportunity to further deepen your understanding using other visual and experiential media. Be careful, because some of these assignments may even be fun!

The second purpose of this companion text is to let you meet other experts in the field of youth ministry. You'll do this through the appendixes and be directed to read them as you read through Robbins' text.

A WORD TO THOSE WHO TEACH

As I stand in front of my classes week by week, I look for ways to make use of the well-known EPIC acronym. I want the pedagogy in my classroom to facilitate learning that is experiential, participatory, image-based, and connective. Another purpose of this companion book to Robbins' text is to give teachers options when it comes to helping your students process the material in ways that promote learning.

I encourage you to have your students at least read and respond to the case studies presented in each chapter. The nature of the response is your call. You can have your students write their responses to the reflection and discussion questions, but it might be better to guide your students in discussion of the case study questions. If your class is larger than 20, I suggest dividing into small groups which could summarize their discussion for the whole class. Beyond the case study questions, you'll see additional options to help your students deal with the material, such as group projects and web-based learning. If you have Internet access in your classroom along with an LCD, you have the opportunity to show your students the web-related material I suggest.

I'm sure you'll occasionally see a learning activity or option that you might think is not wholly beneficial. I would humbly ask you to think again. We all tend to teach the way we ourselves learn best, to the exclusion of other learning styles. Some of the ideas I suggest are purposefully included to not exclude any of the learning styles, to make sure to engage as many of the divergent interests of your students as possible.

Each of the chapters includes a section of ideas for a major project or paper. Most traditional academic classes have some kind of term paper and a midterm exam. I recommend that you let the students read through all 14 of these final sections in the first week of the semester or quarter, and let them select two or three major projects instead of the traditional term paper and midterm exam.

If you come up with additional creative ways to help your students interact with Robbins' text... great! If you're willing, please e-mail your successful ideas to me (KagelerL@Nyack.edu) and perhaps they can be incorporated into a future edition of this book.

As for the appendixes, Robbins is giving your students the opportunity to look over the shoulders of many experts in the field. His text will trigger the appropriate appendix article for your students to read. You will find a couple of reflection and discussion questions to help your students engage the appendixes as well. Please refer to the Bibliography in the main text for sources cited herein.

CHAPTER 1

DOWN THE GREAT UNKNOWN

WARM UP

If you or your friends are into video games, what game most represents to you the idea of a quest or adventure? In what respect? If shopping is your thing, what do you like to look for that makes it a great (and enjoyable) adventure? If you had a tough time yourself back in high school, what were things that made those years so hard and such a struggle?

Robbins has got us thinking about youth ministry in terms of an adventure. The first three cases illustrate the kind of eager excitement and adventure those who begin this youth ministry journey experience.

CASE STUDIES

Case 1

I was beyond excited. It was finally happening. The moving van, having already unloaded some furniture and other miscellany at our basement apartment, was now at the church unloading my books and files into my office. My office! After all the years of education, summer youth ministry projects, internships, part-time director of this, part-time director of that, I was actually a full-time paid youth pastor.

Some of the kids I had met a few months earlier when I interviewed as a candidate came by to offer their helping hands. The senior pastor and associate pastor, both friends of mine from previous contacts, came by with a smile; and the secretary (a secretary, what a concept! Someone that I could actually give work to!) brought a plate of cookies. For one of the first times in my life I actually felt almost like an adult.

As I arranged my desk and shelves the next day I sometimes paused and just looked out the window. I had a view of the church parking lot, but it was a wonderful view to me because parked there was the church van and the church bus. A bus! I knew myself well enough to know that I would be spending much of my life in those vehicles because I loved to travel with kids. I loved to hike, backpack, ski, and camp with teenagers. "Road trip time" was prime ministry time. I was starting my ministry there in January and was already mentally scheduling winter retreats and a whole series of youth camping, backpacking, and hiking trips. I was in charge of junior high, "young people" (senior high and college combined), and young marrieds.

My enthusiasm and positive attitude were contagious, and the first few days went great. My first setback came on my second Sunday. An adhoc group of older "young people" wanted to meet with me after the morning service. I happily agreed, and they shared their unanimous strong feeling that there needed to be a separate college group, since the needs of 22-year-olds are quite different than the needs of 14-year-olds. I completely agreed. They asked if we could separate the groups now, and I said, "Sure, let's do it!"

I've always found it easy to make decisions without self-doubt or insecurity. Obviously, there was a need for this change to happen; I had a ready-made leadership team willing to help take the ball; and I was the youth pastor, who was supposed to give leadership, so lead I did. By that evening the whole church knew of the decision, and all hell broke loose. (Well, okay, I suppose it wasn't quite that bad, but it was bad.) Some kids called on the phone and screamed at me. Some called in tears. Others called to offer "wise counsel" that I had made a stupid decision. One prominent church family (related, it seems, to about a third of the congregation) threatened to leave the church if the decision wasn't rescinded.

What was the big deal, you ask? I soon learned that the high school age girls were the ones who were angry to the point of hatred. They viewed the college-age guys in the young people's group as "their territory." The high school guys, they felt, were, immature. Of course their concerns were couched in spiritual terms. The girls, it seems, were sure it could not be God's will for the change to take place. Sigh.

If youth ministry were going to be a great adventure indeed, it was going to take some grace to make it happen.

—L.K.

Case 2

The wait was finally over. I found the perfect place for me to minister to young people. I was thrilled to be starting what I knew would be an incredible adventure. It had been over a year since I had graduated from college. It wasn't that I didn't have plenty of opportunities to work as youth pastor, but I really felt that God was telling me to wait. It was so beautiful when the wait was finally over and I found my place.

It was totally God who opened the door for me to work in a parachurch organization that has been ministering to young people on Long Island, New York, for over 30 years. Needless to say, when I first started I was very excited. First of all, to know—through countless confirmations from God—that you are in the place God wants you to be is always exciting. Personally, it was awesome to find an organization that ministers to young people exactly the way I wanted to minister.

I had always felt that God wanted me to reach out to youths who would never set foot into a church. There are over 100 high schools on Long Island, and the majority of students never go to any kind of church service. I had always wanted to minister to that kind of kid. Now I was getting the opportunity.

The whole experience was amazing. I moved into a new apartment in a new town. I had my own office. Granted, I shared it with a few others, but still, it was my desk and my computer. I went to Indiana and Michigan for six weeks of training. That was incredible (and not to mention all paid for). When I returned I started meeting all the people interested in helping the ministry. It was great to meet so many caring adults. Finally, the kids. It was an experience I will never forget. Meeting the kids who would be a core of this ministry was the best part. God was already doing a work here long before I ever showed up. It was amazing and humbling. Everything seemed so right, so perfect.

After almost a year I still love my job. I love ministering to young people. It has not, however, been exactly how I thought it would be. I decided in the second semester to tackle some pretty tough issues with the high school group. We discussed creation, abortion, and homosexuality. It was intense. The group was full of diverse opinions each night. Everything was going great. The students were really being challenged to think and to know what they believed and why they believed it. However, the night we discussed homosexuality something went terribly wrong. I wasn't aware of it until the next night when an involved parent communicated to me that his daughter and two of her friends told him that I was "gay bashing" all night.

I was shocked and crushed. I couldn't sleep all night. I was so upset that I had miscommunicated so badly. My mind went crazy thinking, "What have I done?" "What if they never come back?" "What if they turn away from God?" I had never felt like such a failure. For a week I tortured myself thinking about how I was going to handle this and wondering how these girls were going to react.

Finally it was time to meet again. I went on as planned with the next discussion and talked to the girls afterwards. To my surprise and relief I discovered they were fine. We cleared the whole thing up, and I didn't even jeopardize anyone's salvation. Well, I hope it never happens again, but if it does, it will pass. Thank God! I knew things like this would and will happen. I guess it is all a part of the adventure.

—Craig

Case 3

Imagine walking into the Amazon jungle, being handed a big knife, and being told, perhaps with an encouraging thump or two on the back, "Okay, kid! Your mission is to build a house here. A nice, functional, contemporary-looking, long-lasting house. Go to it!"

Gulp.

My own personal Amazon was a one-year-old church plant in a remote part of the country (the part where it snows eight months of the year, and people regularly eat moose meat). My mission? Creating a youth ministry, along with a few other responsibilities, at this small-but-growing, under-equipped but enthusiastic church, starting with a small contingent of high school students.

Now, I had worked with students before. I loved students! It was the joy of building relationships with teenagers—the road trips, the breakfasts out, the late-night conversations about God and life and the Bible—that had led me to pursue a seminary degree and full-time ministry in the first place. But never before had I been responsible for building the whole house...er, youth ministry, especially in a place where there was no foundation of a previous ministry to build upon.

So, as I met this new group of young people, I was thrilled, energized, and yet mired in confusion over what direction the ministry should take. My mind started running in a hundred directions: Should we be purpose-driven? Worship-driven? Cell group-based? Seeker-sensitive? Believer-focused? Should we have large groups, small groups, prayer groups, fellowship groups, or no groups at all? Should we do sports outreaches? Outreaches for skaters or artists or card-carrying NRA kids? These were the questions that plagued me during my first year of youth ministry.

My pastor's expectations? "Whatever you decide to do is fine!" My own expectations? The attractively-designed, fully functional, all-encompassing, air-conditioned-wall-to-wall-carpeting model that I had heard everyone else was building.

In time, we did find our "groove," so to speak, in the youth ministry. But it didn't happen overnight. We did grow numerically, but not for a while. After I got to know the group better we developed some creative outreaches, like the very low-budget coffeehouse we did once a month—no bands, no cappuccino machines, just a mellow, highly relational environment that the kids and their friends somehow loved. In time, we saw some kids' lives transformed—not when we decided it would happen, but when God decided.

I knew a simple truth in my head before I started, but I truly came to realize it in those first few months and years of youth ministry. Youth ministry is all about God and the students. Programs or no programs, it is purely about the wonderful kids that God brings into the ministry. Strategies or no strategies, it is about God moving in their lives. Big numbers or small numbers, it is God who makes things grow—even houses in the jungle.

—Faith

Reflections on Cases 1, 2, and 3

1) If you have had experience in youth ministry, what are some of the things you have enjoyed?

2) With the case studies in mind, what are some of the positive things about full-time youth ministry you anticipate? What other aspects of youth ministry do you look forward to?

3) Cases 1 and 2 mentioned some early hazards that made the start of their youth ministry experience a challenge. What other early hazards might you foresee, or what early hazards have you already experienced?

Further Reflections on Case 1

4) Regarding the big decision to split the young people's group into high school and college, what would you have done?

5) Given the author's hasty decision, what would you have done in the aftermath if you were in his shoes? What role could grace play?

HERE'S WHAT THE AUTHOR ACTUALLY DID (Case 1):

I decided to stick with the original decision. The group of college-age people who met with me that Sunday did their best to show support and gratitude. I tried to mollify the high school girls by allowing college age guys to come to the high school group from then (January) through the coming summer (none did). I explained the wisdom of my decision to the church's Christian Ed. committee, highlighting adolescent development and ministry implications. They had been lobbied hard by the anti-decision forces, but they voted to support the change. Some of the high school girls never did forgive me. The high school guys were happy about the decision because now they had these girls without competition from older guys, at least during group time. But it was a very tough rest of the school year with the high school group. Attendance was way down and it was hard to generate any sense of positiveness. And the threatening family, well, they visibly reduced their involvement in the church and eventually stopped coming altogether.

FOR FURTHER DISCUSSION:

College Seniors Talk About Getting into Youth Ministry

The following college seniors (youth ministry majors) are responding to two questions: 1) What are a couple of things that have really excited you in your youth ministry experience so far? and 2) What are you eagerly anticipating when you finally graduate and can do this full time?

Katie: I think the things that get me most excited now about being in youth ministry are the answers to prayer I have seen. Big ones like a 12-year-old's healing from terminal cancer and "smaller" ones, like an 18-year-old learning to truly love and appreciate her younger brother. God's love and care for the kids in my ministry and their seemingly petty concerns bring joy to me as I see him changing their hearts and lives. I am also really looking forward to not having so many constraints on my time and all the added drama and stress that school brings. I'm looking forward to having a home that I can invite kids to and just having tons of time to be with them.

Rob: I love teaching the Bible and hanging out with kids. I'm really looking forward to full-time youth ministry when I can develop a ministry that reaches kids where they are. And I love mission trips! That's going to be a blast. I want to enjoy time with the kids and raise up leaders in the church. I can't wait to see one kid's life changed. I've seen it in the past—those moments where kids let down all their guard and allow Jesus in, and then down the road they've still got it. It's great when you see a hard, broken kid change into a passionate lover of Christ.

Matt: One of the things that has made me excited is being able to come up with new and creative ideas for youth group and ministry. Another is discovering that video can be put on CDs and finding that I have a gift to do this tech stuff. It's in the tech side of ministry where I feel God showing me this is what he made me for. It all began in my sophomore year when I picked up my first video-editing program. It's cool to step right into the plans God has for your life. I'm excited to bring Jesus Christ to people in a way that is different and creative and capturing. I'm excited to bring all that Christ is to multimedia. He used parables to communicate. The tech side of ministry is like using parables.

Joanna: I love it when my kids grasp the reality of a personal relationship with Christ and take the next step and tell others. Another reason I enjoy my ministry is the opportunity to disciple the female students on the ride home from our weekly Bible studies. I am eagerly waiting for the time when God gives me the signal to walk up in front of other women in ministry to encourage them. I believe God wants me to help other women in ministry in encouragement, healing, and with joy. There are many female students who need another woman to come alongside and mentor them.

Mike: I love teaching the Bible and really seeing kids learn and understand an aspect of God or their relationship that they didn't before. I love the one-on-one stuff too. Being able to really get into this full time will mean I can give it my full attention and loose my passion for it. Up to this point I have had to not be as passionate about ministry as I could because I had a lot of other things, like work and school, that took time and energy. I knew I couldn't be as focused on ministry as I wanted to be. Soon I'll be able to run with the calling God has for me 100 percent.

Paul: One thing I love to do is spend time with students outside of youth group. I've really been noticing how different some students are when you get them alone. One guy, Allen, is an obnoxious middle schooler at youth group with his friends, but when I meet with him I see how much he has matured. I love that! I'm getting better at knowing how to reach middle schoolers, both in teaching and in being present with them.

As I look ahead to full time, I'm getting excited about a chance to really develop my vision and focus the ministry. Being a student, I feel I really don't have the time to step back and think about the purpose and direction of the ministry. When I'm full time I plan to have time set apart just for developing and evaluating that vision.

Sun Yun: One thing that makes me sing "Kumbaya" happened just this last Sunday. I preached, and after preaching one of my students came up to me and handed me a vanilla milk and said "Thank you for the good sermon!" Then she gave me a hug. I love it also when I see students ministering to students. I'm so looking forward to having more time for ministry. I won't have to think about a deadline for homework that I might not be very interested in.

Greg: I love the one-on-one discipleship chances I get before and after youth group. I feel God's hand of blessing when a student approaches me so I can pray for them or give them advice about an issue. Something about speaking their names followed by a word of blessing makes me so happy I'm doing this work.

There is just something about having my own office in the future that makes me very excited! Big cushy chair, walls covered with ministry books, and an L-shaped desk...ah, the warm fuzzies!

Reflections on Student Statements

6) What are some common elements of these statements?

7) Which statement do you most identify with? In what respect?

8) Though not stated, these students feel God calling them into youth ministry. How is it that you yourself feel led or called into youth ministry? Robbins brings up 2 Corinthians 5:18-21. What biblical connection or anchor can you make to your sense of call?

DISCUSSION ABOUT MOTIVATIONS TO BE IN YOUTH MINISTRY

The subjective motivation to be in youth ministry is perhaps not as lofty as the notion of God's divine calling, but it is an important subject. It helps people begin the journey as well as keeping them on it.

9) From Robbins' chapter, the case studies, and the student statements, what right or even possibly wrong motives can you begin to see?

10) According to Paul Borthwick in his *Feeding Your Forgotten Soul*, wrong motives for youth ministry include enhancing self-esteem, being "cool," and experiencing power over others. Other wrong motives would be money or sex. What, do you think, would be some of the long-term fruit of those in ministry who have these or other wrong motives for youth ministry? When you were younger, were you ever in a youth ministry whose leadership you now see had motives that were not entirely good? How did you know and how did that make you feel?

11) What are some right motives for youth ministry? Which of these right motives is the closest expression of where your own heart is?

Ideas for a major project or paper

1) Find a group of youth workers to survey with these questions: How did you get into youth ministry in the first place? What makes you willing to put up with all the hard things about youth ministry and still do it? See what similarities you find among your survey respondents and what connections you see between those responses and those found in Chapter One.

2) Prepare an annotated Internet bibliography of at least 10 entries on the subject of "God's calling into youth ministry." A google.com search will result in over 80,000 web pages, some of which are fascinating first-hand accounts.

3) Produce a collection of movie or TV clips that illustrate either a) beginning an adventure, b) a defining moment (like a "call") where a character is transformed and sets out on a quest or noble task, or c) examples of right or wrong motives for action. (Be sure to make a copy of this production to give to your professor so he or she can appear "cutting edge" when talking about this in another class.)

CHAPTER 2

A JOURNEY MARKED BY "BLAZES"

WARM UP

Think of arenas of life where success requires focus. Can you think of sports examples? How about in academics? What other areas can you think of that require focus for success? This chapter calls us to remember that ministry is, after all, a spiritual activity that requires a spiritual focus. Also, youth ministry is solidly connected to other areas of knowledge that we must understand if we're to proceed on the adventure.

CASE STUDIES

Case 4

When I started in youth ministry I knew it was important for me to have a close relationship with God, because, after all, how could I expect kids in my youth group to be any closer to him than I was? Yet at first it was very difficult to carve out time to have this close relationship. I thought I was a spiritual giant because I spent 15-30 minutes a day in the Bible and did my praying on the run—either while literally running (for exercise) or when driving. (I had a deal with God that I would pray on the way to some place and listen to music on the way back.)

The reason I couldn't take the time for longer devotional time or more prayer time was that everything else in the ministry took so much time. My first retreat, six weeks after I arrived, took more than 20 hours to prepare for. I worked hard on my preparation for youth Bible studies, youth talks, Sunday school lessons, and discipleship times. Each one would take hours. Of course there also were the expectations that I would be out with the kids after school and on weekends.

But you know what? Over time, I got better at preparation. As I said, my first retreat took 20 hours to get ready for, but my tenth retreat took about five, and (years later) my thirtieth took about three. And the thirtieth retreat was far better than the first—same thing with Bible studies, discipleship, Sunday school, and other preps. With experience, they took less time.

I was at my first church only three years, but after three years at my second church, I was able to take the first two hours of almost every day at the office for personal and spiritual refreshment. I did this with the full support of the senior pastor. His reasoning was that the congregation didn't expect its pastors to be spiritually "average," so it made sense to build personal and spiritual growth time into my normal day. I set it up with the receptionist to field phone calls for me from 8 a.m. to 10 a.m. by saying, "He's not available right now. Can he call you at 10?" I was getting paid to spend time with God! How cool is that?

I eventually found a good pattern that went like this: First, I prayed for kids and the youth ministry. (I continued to pray for personal and family stuff earlier in the morning when I did my running.) Then I had some good time in the Word. I usually went through the Bible one book at a time, taking notes along the lines of three questions: What does it say? What does it mean? How does it apply to me? I kept a couple of good commentaries close at hand and read them as well. I wanted to be biblically literate, but I also wanted to remember that the Word was meeting God, not for knowledge only.

That study would finish out the first hour. Then I would go to the one comfortable chair I had in my office, put on some music, and just read. I read youth ministry stuff—magazines, journals, and the latest books. I also needed to get better at management, so I read a lot of books on leadership and administration. I read books on the church and on change. Anything, even hobby-type books, was fair game for that second hour.

And what if I got sleepy during that two-hour period? I took a 15-minute "power nap" right there on my floor or in my comfy chair! Fortunately I don't snore, so no one passing in the hall would know that I was sound asleep. To wake up I'd grab a Diet Coke or Mountain Dew out of the office fridge, and I was good to go again.

This personal Bible study and reading program has really influenced my life over the years. My wife and I are accountable to tell each other what we've had for devotions that day, so that keeps me thinking about the Word during the day. (It's really embarrassing to not be able to remember!)

As for the reading of other books, I log them into my journal on a special page. (By the way, I journal about once a week, reflecting on the "lived moments" of the past week, when I felt most fully alive.) At the end of the year, I take my journal to Starbucks (usually) and have a cerebral "books of the year" ceremony in which I declare in my journal which were the three best books of the year. It's quite fun, actually, and encouraging to see how little pieces of some of these books have continued to mold me and influence who I am.

The spiritual growth from this time with God and the Word helps my students understand that I want to grow spiritually as well. I'm not an expert whose sole purpose is to have them listen to and benefit from my vast knowledge and maturity. Nope, I'm a fellow disciple, trying to figure out how to live the life day to day. I have joy in sharing with them something special that came up in my devotions, and some of them have joy in sharing how their own walks with God have energized and brought meaning to them as well.

—L.K.

Case 5

It never seems to fail. Whenever I am overextended and feel swamped, a crisis strikes. One time I was approaching the deadline for our summer missions trip, and the deposit was due within a week, and I only had three registrations. I still had a to-do list a mile long for our big outreach the coming weekend, and I had not prepared at all for our mid-week discipleship meeting. Then the phone rang, and it was a distressed parent upset about her teenage daughter's bad attitude. She wanted to come in and talk about this, at length. How I respond in situations like this says something about how healthy my relationship with Christ is.

I am wired to be on the go; being around people energizes me. I hate to sit still and dread to be alone. I thrive when I am able to multitask, and I search for challenges that will ensure busyness. When I am facing downtime I often find myself looking for the TV remote, flipping on the radio, or heading to my computer hoping for e-mail or a buddy online to chat with. It is often during the period of most stress that I feel the most fulfilled. However, this has also been the driest time of my life. If my spiritual well is not filled, I lose focus and minister out of my strengths instead of out of Christ in me.

I learned early in ministry how to recognize if I am out of balance. When life gets crazy, the areas I neglect the most are those that seem the most secure. In other words, my tendency is to continue working hard in the ministry and overlook my relationship with my wife. I realize that if my relationship with her, which is tangible, suffers because of ministry, my relationship with Christ also suffers. To bring balance and health back to my marriage I must stop the busyness and focus on my wife by spending time with her alone. I also must stop and be still before God. It is in this time of quietness where I am completely still that intimacy with Christ is cultivated. The challenge I face is to create this time daily and not to wait until I am out of balance.

My view of the Bible's role in all of this has really changed over the years. For years the Bible was merely a source of knowledge and wisdom. It has been through the pains and pressures of ministry that the Word has been both reassuring as well as transformational. I have truly experienced the power of the living Word. I no longer read the Bible merely to gain knowledge so that I will be able speak authoritatively on any topic; instead it is a place where I experience the life-giving words of a loving and just Father.

—Doug

Case 6

If I had to describe in one word my attempts to stay spiritually focused over the first two years of my ministry, it would probably be "inconsistent."

There are periods of time when I'm on the money, keeping up with some sort of personal time of worship and study on nearly a daily basis. There are other periods of time when I struggle to have time with God just once a week, or worse. As I grow more experienced as a youth pastor, I realize the need to become more disciplined, and so I think over time the ability to remain steadfast in personal time with God has become easier to achieve. It has become my true desire to worry about my relationship with God first, because if mine is growing, helping others to grow will just fall into place. In my ups and downs, there are several things I find important to help keep me spiritually focused and motivated.

First of all, my number one priority and loyalty is to God. I have a clear understanding with the staff relations committee and elders that this is my main focus. They support me by encouraging personal spiritual study right there at my office and they expect me to take "spiritual retreats" at least once a year.

Prayer is becoming huge in my life. I'm praying for a continued hunger and desire for God to be within me. I pray that I won't be satisfied with ministry unless I'm responding to this hunger and desire regularly, on a daily basis, even multiple times daily. I'm realizing more and more how necessary it is to have God be a part of all aspects of my day. There are so many little things that come up during the day that tend to get me off focus.

One way I kind of watch myself in regard to prayer and intimacy to Christ is this: if all my "spare" time is spent in sports and hobbies and with my girlfriend, and I devote nothing of my extra energy to my spiritual life, something is upside down! Right now I've structured two main devotion and worship times in my day. One of these is when I first get in to work and another is at night right before I go to bed. Having a time at work and a time at home is good because it helps me keep an emphasis on growing both as a minister and personally. And, if I miss one, which does happen, I have another one planned to make up for it. I expect to be married some time in the future, so perhaps the evening time is one I could do with my wife.

Another thing that has helped me stay spiritually focused is to attend conferences and conventions. It's nice having the church pay for these things. I really get into the worship times and seek out sessions that will deepen me with God. I learn stuff too, of course, but it's just inspiring and encouraging to be with so many other people with the same love for the Lord and youth. I try to keep the TV off in the hotel room too, so God can speak to me there if he wants.

Every few months I try to get away just by myself for a day, just to have my own spiritual retreat. Sitting in youth ministry classes at college, it never occurred to me how important it would be to be in a church that was concerned that I be spiritually healthy, and willing to help me get there. I'm thankful I'm in one!

—Joe

Reflections on Cases 4, 5, and 6

1) What are some of the common barriers to a focus on God expressed in these cases?

2) Which of these barriers do you see as a challenge for you as you anticipate ministry? How so?

3) Of the various ways to maintain focus on God mentioned in the cases, which do you think will be a good fit for you? Can you think of others?

FOR FURTHER DISCUSSION:

Connection of Youth Ministry to Other Academic Disciplines

Duffy Robbins makes a great case for both awareness and understanding of the links between other fields of study and the practice of youth ministry. Here is a case where the youth worker carried his understanding of postmodernism, which is a common subject in both philosophy and sociology, to his understanding of personal evangelism with early adolescents.

Case 7

I knew that kids today are more and more postmodern in their thinking. As a result of this I've taken quite a different approach to personal evangelism with kids.

Jill was invited to our junior high group by a regular attender of the group, and she seemed to enjoy it. She came back regularly for several months, and I got to know her better through hang-out time and playing all the games that our middle-schoolers like to play: amoeba tag, capture the flag, shuffle your buns, sit-down-backwards basketball, volleyball, and so on. It quickly became apparent that Jill was not from a Christian background. She seemed to know every lyric of every song about sex that has ever been written in any language. She enjoyed rattling off the lurid lyrics of songs in the hearing of some of our home-school kids who also attend regularly, just to watch the shock on their faces. Her clothes fit as if she had been poured into them, and she was the typical "12-year-old going on 20" in appearance.

Anyway, I was leading the Bible study portion of our weekly meeting, and out of the blue she raised her hand and asked, "Will I go to hell if I have sex before marriage?" This was way off the topic of the night, to say the least, and I told her I'd answer her later. During refreshment time she asked me again. Now, years earlier I would have used the opportunity that night to present her a major explanation of the biblical view of sex and lead right into something along the lines of "Jill, God loves you and has a wonderful plan for your life..." But I didn't. I just said, "Good question; bring it up again in a week or two." She looked a little befuddled by this response and walked off.

The next week she sought me out as soon as I arrived. "Will I go to hell if I have sex before marriage?" My answer? "Well, Jill, whether or not you go to heaven or hell kinda depends on who you know, not what you do." And with that I walked off to play ping-pong with some of the guys. Again, her eyes were wide in confusion.

The next week I approached her. "So, Jill, have you figured it out yet?"

"No, I don't have a clue."

Then I gave her a few sentences about knowing Jesus, and again, I walked away just leaving her standing there.

Two weeks passed and the group was playing frozen tag on the basketball court. I happened to be "frozen" about five feet from where Jill was similarly frozen.

"Say, Jill, do you know God yet?"

"I'm afraid."

"Good, I think you're getting close." And the game continued as first she, then I, became "unfrozen."

Later that evening someone else on the staff was doing the Bible study part. Jill raised her hand in the middle and actually asked, "How do you know Jesus?" Mark, who was leading, said, "Good question," and let some of the other students there answer it.

What's so amazing is what happened afterwards. Brent is a guy who was then 12 and looked like he was only nine. Most of the time it seems that in his head the lights are on, but no one is home. Well, that night, someone was home. Right after the meeting ended he took Jill into a side Sunday School room, explained the plan of salvation to her, and prayed with her to receive Christ! She came out in tears of joy and over the weeks we all saw a complete transformation in her. She was no longer cold, hard, "edgy," and proudly sexual. We all watched the fruit of the Spirit begin to form in her life.

—L.K.

Reflections on Case 7

4) What is your understanding of postmodernism? (Not sure? There are some good summations on google.com)

5) In what respect was the youth worker in case 7 doing personal evangelism in a postmodern way?

6) What do you see as the possible risks or potential benefits of the approach he took?

7) See if you can think of anything in any of your other non-youth ministry classes where you see a good link between that class and the practice of youth ministry.

Ideas For a Major Project or Paper

1) Compare and contrast the helpfulness to you of five free online devotionals. A google.com search for "daily devotionals" will yield ample hits. Try several for several days each and compare them with criteria such as: a) connecting me to the Word, b) application to my personal life, and c) potential application especially to those in ministry.

2) Do the same as in idea 1, but use devotional books instead.

3) On page 36-37 Robbins lists some pretty horrible issues brought to him by one of his graduates. Choose one of these issues and interview five full-time youth pastors about the issue. What wise counsel were you able to glean? Alternatively, write a major paper on one of the topics listed. Use this paper to arm yourself if you have a similar experience.

Unit 1:
Journey From the Inside Out

CHAPTER 3

THE CALL OF THE WILD

WARM UP

When you were a child, what did the term "pastor" mean to you? What images come to mind or what feelings can you recall having about one of the pastors in your life when you were growing up?

CASE STUDIES

Case 8

I was raised in a small Baptist church, but we did have a youth group, and it was actually a pretty good one. We did a lot of stuff in addition to our weekly meetings, and pretty much everything was planned by a leadership group of kids. One of the big tragedies of my junior high youth group years had to do with Charlene. I was intending to sit next to her on the long drive to our annual day at the ocean, and I fully expected by the end of the day we would be boyfriend and girlfriend. The night before, though, I was hit in the face by a horseshoe (long story!) and spent the next day in dental surgery. I missed the ocean day, and Charlene and I never did get together. Sigh! In early high school my dominant concern was Sheila, also in the youth group. If I was elected to the youth council, my main concern was that she be on it, too. Sheila eventually dumped me and started going out with my best friend, so that put a little damper on the warm fuzziness of our youth group for awhile.

Despite these relational setbacks, I had good youth group experiences as an adolescent. Though those experiences were often dominated by guy-girl concerns, I did grow spiritually and was given opportunity to practice leadership. As for my view of pastors, well, it did begin to change. Up until around age 14 I thought you had to have two things to be a pastor. Number one, and most important, is that you had to be really old. And a close second, you had to be really boring. But then an amazing thing happened. Our little church got a new pastor. He was 28, vigorous, and he knew how to ski. He knew how to ski! I mean, never in my life had I dreamed pastors did normal things, like skiing. And his wife was gorgeous. Yikes, I never dreamed I'd ever have to try hard not to have lustful thoughts about my pastor's wife! Anyway, for the first time in my life I had before me an example of people who were in "full-time ministry" and having a blast in the process. Not long afterwards I had an inner sense that I should go into the ministry too. Pastor Mark took me skiing one time and said he could see me in the ministry. I could, too!

I guess the leaders of the local Youth for Christ saw potential in me (they told me so), and they proved it by offering me the position of Director of Junior High Outreach when I graduated from high school. They said it was a paid position, but I wouldn't accept the money, I was so honored and thrilled to do something for God. So, while I attended university and lived 30 miles away, I ran a monthly junior high rally program in my hometown. I recruited, from area churches, about 20 people to help staff it, and over those four years we had some great programs, some real flops, and we saw many kids come to Christ.

In my second year of university I added to my ministry plate a Director of Junior High Ministry position at a church about a mile from where I lived. Now, at last, I could have more personal contact with kids and do relational ministry, instead of just managing a program like I did for YFC. I was the only staff person with the kids, and they all lived close to the church, so I could make a few phone calls and in 30 minutes have 20 or 30 kids waiting for me at the park next to the church to play soccer or football, or fly kites. We had such a great time, and I felt God's smile on this. I do thank God that in his mercy we did not have any major tragedies. The police officer who pulled me over when I had 13 (!) middle schoolers packed into my Camaro didn't think I was nearly as cool as the kids did. And it did occur to me, when during a river-rafting trip that I had no business leading, a kid came very close to drowning, that perhaps I should think a little harder about safety issues.

After a year and a half the group had grown to about 70 regulars, but they were all pretty shallow spiritually. We started some discipleship emphasis and many of those kids actually grew deep in Christ and made a real impact on their high school when they got older.

During the summers I directed a high school Christian drop-in center and eventually it was supported financially by 20 area churches. People told me I not only had pastoral gifts but leadership and administrative gifts as well.

I assumed my "call into the ministry" meant that I should be a preaching pastor, so I went to seminary. I fondly remembered my university youth ministry days as valuable. "It will be good when I'm a pastor to know how to help youth staff do their job," I thought. My main ministry experience during seminary was again in youth ministry

At the ripe old age of 25 I graduated from seminary with an M.Div. but, at least in the Baptist denomination I was part of, you're really not old enough to be a senior pastor at age 25. So...I did what I knew best: I became a youth pastor. After a very rough start, things began to flourish, and it occurred to me that perhaps youth ministry was, for me at least, not a stepping stone, a purgatory, or a hoop to jump through en route to the "real" ministry, but the real thing. In working with youth it seemed I was doing what I was born to do.

I was a full-time youth pastor for 20 years, and am now a volunteer worker in a junior high ministry while I teach youth ministry full-time at a college.

—L.K.

Case 9

Here are some statements by current youth pastors answering this question: What does it mean to you to be called into youth ministry?

"Recognizing giftedness and ability; receiving direction and commendation from godly mentors, friends, elders, and pastors; asking the Spirit for direction; and maybe being available and willing to meet a current youth ministry need and thereby 'falling' into it."

"Going through doors God produces for you."

"God has prepared me to be in this work. I feel God's pleasure in me being in this work. It means the work is effective even if I don't see the effects."

"When everything else you do doesn't quench your thirst."

"God places a burden on your heart for young lives. If that happens, you do youth ministry wherever you are, no matter what the situation, paid or not."

"Couldn't imagine doing anything else, even if the calling is a love-hate thing."

"It's a vision, a passion, a compassionate leading of God toward young people that is a persistent knocking."

"To be created for youth ministry...given the heart, love, and desire. It's like a marriage relationship."

"To have a deep burden, a heart that bleeds for youth and their needs, especially their spiritual welfare."

"To be a servant-friend of young people in the power of Christ."

"To love kids and their world, their hurts, their joys, their needs."

"To be transparent and allow Christ to flow through me to the end of salvation, discipleship, and spiritual growth."

"Discipling youth, modeling faith, building bridges."

Reflections on Cases 8 and 9

In case 8, it looks as if several things contributed to the writer's sense of call into youth ministry: a) a good experience as a teenager in a church youth group, b) a good role model in ministry, c) opportunities to minister that went well, d) strategic affirmations along the way, and e) a divine sense of God's pleasure in it all.

1) Which of the above five experiences (a-e) can you identify with? In what way?

2) Are there other "contributors to call" that you can think of from your own life or the lives of others you know? (For example, some have had a horrendous adolescence; calling into youth ministry involves helping kids not make the same mistakes or experiencing the same things.) In what respect can you identify with these you've listed?

3) In case 8, what are one or two experiences that you personally found the most interesting? Why?

4) Go back through all the statements in case 9. What are two or three you most identify with? Why?

FOR FURTHER DISCUSSION:

Youth Pastoral Leadership

5) Thinking about leadership basics in Chapter 3, come up with a movie clip illustration for each of those that Robbins listed (steward, herald, witness, father, servant). Be prepared to explain the application of your clip to leadership.

6) Divide the class into three debate teams. Prepare a class debate based on Robbins' three notions of leadership. Each team takes one of the notions (chain of command, sharing, and servant) and is prepared to argue its merits biblically and practically.

7) Deepen your understanding of Swain's Four Leadership Styles (sovereign, parallel, mutual, and servanthood, described in Chapter 3) by preparing a short skit for each one or its opposite.

8) Fill in the rest of Chapter 3's "Observations from John 10:1-18" chart.

Ideas for a Major Project or Paper

1) One of the statements in case 9 identifies calling as a "love-hate" thing. Explore this notion. First, take a look at some Old Testament prophets and the New Testament apostles. You'll find ample examples of things about the call to both love and hate. Next, pick a couple of people you know and respect who are in full-time ministry. Learn what it is they love about being in the ministry. Is there anything they hate about it? Finally, have you had any experiences of a love-hate calling to ministry? Process these in light of the first two steps in this project description.

2) Explore some of the leadership resources on the Internet. On google.com, click on "advanced search" and enter "leadership styles" in the exact words field. Prepare a detailed description of at least five resources that come up, and suggest for each the application (or not) to youth ministry pastoral leadership.

3) Dig deeper into the idea of servant leadership. The most comprehensive secular site on the topic is The Greenleaf Center for Servant Leadership (greenleaf.org). a) Prepare, 5-10 page paper on the topic of servant leadership, including its biblical aspects. b) Prepare another expression of servant leadership concepts through other visual media (art, still photography, dance, and so on).

4) Prepare an annotated bibliography on the subject of Christian ministry leadership with at least 10 entries. A good place to start would be amazon.com, with a "Christian Ministry Leadership" entry.

5) Obtain (perhaps in association with other class members) either through purchase, interlibrary loan, or your own college library 10 good books on Christian ministry leadership. Briefly survey each book and determine one concept from each book that you think is most helpful and applicable to youth ministry leadership.

CHAPTER 4

Through Many Dangers, Toils, and Snares

WARM UP

Tell about a time you were in actual physical danger. For example, have you ever almost drowned, fallen off a cliff, or fallen asleep while driving? In your example, to what extent were you, now that you think about it, at fault?

CASE STUDIES

Case 10

I love backpacking, but early on, even at the time, this one seemed like a nightmare. I guess that's a little strong, but right away it just started going bad.

I normally allow no more than 12 high school kids, plus me and two other staff, to come on any one trip. That's what we had, but I gave in to the pleas of six college-age guys who wanted to come along too. They said they would not (at least in theory) hike with the group or even camp for the night where we would camp. They promised I would have to give no thought to them, and they were not my responsibility (in their eyes or the eyes of the church or their parents). That fine arrangement broke down the first night when very bad weather moved in on us in a hurry. The college guys didn't have enough gear to keep warm and dry in a severe storm, so they were with us from then on.

This was 100% distracting to the girls on the trip, some of whom imagined themselves in wonderful romantic relationships with these guys. And of course, wouldn't it be romantic if their relationship began in the natural beauty of mountain and glacial grandeur? What could be better? Keeping warm by the fire with that special guy, a leisurely good-night kiss, or perhaps "sleeping" together in a cozy tent or out under the stars if it ever did stop raining—a dream come true, right? A nightmare if you're a youth pastor trying to have kids come back without gaining sexual experience or even a pregnancy! So some of the kids were very upset at me for always spoiling their fun. Others were upset at me for allowing the guys to come along in the first place. Our trips had become famous for real spiritual highpoints and deep community, neither of which were happening this time around. This trip turned into a war zone instead.

Speaking of war zones, I soon had the federal government against me too. The park rangers who patrolled the high country were drop-jawed disbelieving with our group size (now 21 in number). This was more than double what they prefer, and their party size limits are well publicized and strictly enforced. I had called weeks ahead of time and gotten grudging approval from them for 10 to 12 youth and three adults, but now we were well beyond that.

By the third night I was so tired of trying to keep the trip functioning, so tired of complaining kids, so tired of zealous park rangers, that I could hardly wait to come home. I was so tired of making decisions about people's moral and physical safety that I was absolutely exhausted emotionally.

On the morning of the last full day in the backcountry, the college-age guys started jumping off a 55-foot cliff into the lake. When I found out, my first thought was, "I couldn't care less." Of course, as you might expect (but it did not occur to me), now the peer pressure was for everyone to do it. The high school guys did. No problem. Jenn and Andrea did, too. Big problem! Both girls were injured, and Jenn required immediate medical evacuation for internal injuries. Like I said, it was a bad trip.

Later that day I was leading the rest of the group (one staff and one kid had gone with Jenn) to the final night's overnight camping spot, which was halfway back to the church bus from our lakeside accident. It was pouring rain, howling wind. We were all wet, miserable, and worried about Jenn who was, by now we hoped, in a hospital. I grieved over my poor decisions on the trip. I grieved over my inability to intervene and stop the cliff jumping. I determined I would accept full responsibility for what happened and began mentally composing the letter to the parents and church board that had to be written. The letter I sent included the following:

"Parents need to feel assured that whoever is in charge will preclude accidents that are clearly avoidable. I let you down this time, and I do not know how to convey the depth of my regret over the decision I made and the injuries that resulted. You would think I would be a little smarter after all the trips I've led. I have no alibis, no excuses; I simply seek your forgiveness."

I went on to explain we would immediately form (with the blessing of the pastor and board) a parent committee on safety guidelines. All future backcountry trips would meet these guidelines, no matter who was leading, no exceptions.

Well, most parents did forgive me, especially Jenn's. Andrea's mother never did forgive me, I don't think, and was always negative about the ministry after that.

—L.K.

Case 11

Things didn't go very well at my third church as a full-time youth pastor. When I interviewed at the church, the congregation was at a regular worship attendance of around 800 and they expected to be over 1,000 within the year. They were looking for a youth pastor who would be more a "rancher" than a shepherd. That is, they knew their youth groups were too big already for just a shepherd; they needed someone who was able to shepherd the shepherds. They sought someone to supply the vision, heart, and passion to motivate the volunteer staff and key youth. It was an exciting opportunity and a great match, it seemed, for my gift mix. The high school group was pretty dysfunctional, and that was actually one of the reasons I felt so strongly I should go. I knew it would force me to grow and be on my knees a lot.

By dysfunctional, I mean things like this: They routinely swore at each other in anger before, during, and after youth group events. They were famous for making guest speakers cry, they were so disrespectful. We had a handful of guys like John, who was just mean-spirited. One night he took special delight in stealing the beautiful watermelon that Keith (who was mentally retarded) had brought to the pool party. John smashed it to smithereens on the road in front of the house and denied that he had done so to me despite the eyewitness accounts of other kids. Keith was heartbroken; John thought it was hilarious. A few months later when one of our staff suggested to John's parents that he might be on drugs, the parents became very upset at me, the youth pastor. It was my fault! Go figure. Our youth group invited a small Baptist church's high school group to come play floor hockey for a night. Our guys mauled their team, and it was a miracle we didn't send Baptist kids to the hospital that night. They went home with cuts and bruises and a "never again" commitment about doing stuff with our youth group. Even though I'd been a youth pastor already for 17 years, I was experiencing things I'd never experienced before.

But you know, after grad Sunday, when John and some of his buddies were no longer in the group, and after six months of discipling, prayer, and trying to put the principles of Sonlife and Purpose Driven into practice, we were definitely turning a corner.

Unfortunately, in the larger church scene, all was not well. Eighteen months after my arrival the church had "grown" from over 800 to fewer than 550. Many families, including families with youth, had left the church, so the youth groups were much smaller. Now they most needed a shepherd youth pastor, not a "rancher" youth pastor. Yes, I can counsel kids, go to the games, hang out with kids for hours, et cetera, et cetera, but that is not my strength. (It occurred to me that the very best person to be the youth pastor at that church would be the other guy who was a candidate 18 months earlier. At the time, they chose me. Now, I was quite sure, what they really needed was his gifting and heart.) I soon found another position, and announced in April that I was resigning and would be done at the end of July, after we finished some key camps and outreaches we had already planned. This scenario was fine with the pastor and the elder chairman, with whom I had consulted throughout the decision-making process.

When my resignation hit the CE committee, one person, a corporate executive, said something along these lines: "He can't possibly be here the next four months with a good attitude. He'll bad-mouth us to the kids and parents. Let's buy out his contract and have him clean out his desk this week. Let's fire him!" The elder chairman was at the meeting and told the guy to shut up, that he knew my character had enough integrity to finish well. (The guy did shut up. This is how things worked at this church, since the elder chair was board chair for a multibillion-dollar-a-year corporation and the let's-fire-him guy was only a vice president of a less than a billion-a-year company.)

The last four months actually went very well. I worked hard to build the group and prepare them for my successor (who was, in fact, the other guy mentioned above), and we had a lot of good times and deep experiences of the Lord and community. I was positive with the kids and parents and was able to stand up and help lead worship each week and feel God's smile. I left there with few regrets and was genuinely happy for their future with their new youth pastor. Sometimes I think about some of the what-ifs, but all in all I feel we ended well for God's glory and the good of the group.

—L.K

Reflections on Cases 10 and 11

Robbins' chapter begins with notions of character and blamelessness. The author of cases 10 and 11 isn't claiming blamelessness, but there are some things about character that come through.

1) Where do you see the author's character in the two cases?

2) Robbins speaks of authenticity. Where do you see authenticity in these cases?

3) In what respects have you seen issues of character or authenticity affect (for good or ill) other youth workers (or pastors) whom you have known? Be specific, but don't reveal names.

4) In your own life and whatever ministry experiences you have had to date, have you seen the need for good character? Blamelessness? Authenticity? Cite at least one specific example for each.

FOR FURTHER DISCUSSION:

Five Danger Areas

5) Come up with five short skits that illustrate these five dangers (Phony Persona, Professional Holiness, Consuming Activity, Dishonest Intimacy, Neglected Relationships).

6) Other than "Dishonest Intimacy" (which we will get to), in what way have you seen the danger area harm someone in the ministry or the ministry itself?

7) Which of the danger areas do you feel most prone towards, given your own personality, background, and internal wiring?

8) On a more positive note, which of the danger areas do you have a good handle on now? In other words, where do you feel strong, perhaps even to the point where you could help another person who was struggling in that particular area?

A FRANK WORD ABOUT SEXUAL MISCONDUCT

Even with the prevalence of clergy sexual abuse in the news these days, it may come as a surprise to some that sexual misconduct is a huge problem in church youth ministry. Churches face lawsuits; people end up in jail; lives, marriages, and careers are ruined more often than anyone wants to acknowledge.

It's not just male youth pastors getting involved sexually with the girls in their group. Female pastors sleep with the guys; staffers have affairs with other staffers; and then there's gay sex. Every few years I hear about a youth pastor who has committed suicide. I sadly say to myself, "It's probably about sex." I heard about one just last year. He was a well-loved and respected youth pastor in a wonderful, growing church on the West Coast. A denominational executive told me some months after, "It wasn't just about sex, it was about gay sex."

Sexual misconduct came up as a major reason youth pastors lose their jobs in my study of 185 youth pastors who'd been fired from their ministries (*The Youth Minister's Survival Guide*, Grand Rapids: Zondervan, 1992). Here are just two examples, with the names changed, of course.

Lynn worked with the high school youth group with her husband, Jerry, the youth pastor. Unfortunately, their marriage was deteriorating. Lynn had sexual relations with two of the guys in the youth group and eventually ran off with one of them. Then Jerry had an affair with one of the youth ministry interns.

Kent fell in love with the senior pastor's daughter and began having sex with her (first on a youth retreat) when she was 16. Their ongoing affair was a secret for a year. When it was discovered, Kent's wife divorced him, and he was fired from his ministry. He left vowing to return one day for his "one true love." Even a year later, after another church hired him as youth pastor, he maintains contact with the pastor's daughter and plans to come back for her.

9) What are some of the emotions you feel when you learn of the existence of sexual misconduct in youth ministry?

10) If you are personally aware of a case, try to reflect and list some of the danger signs you may have observed before things became public. Have you ever had the unhappy task of "blowing the whistle"? (For example, I eventually confronted a youth pastor older than myself who was full-contact wrestling with a "mature" girl in his group. I observed this behavior on four separate occasions, was deeply troubled by it, and finally blew the whistle.)

11) Why do you think sexual misconduct is such a problem in youth ministry?

12) Generally, youth pastors do not intentionally plan to engage in sexual misconduct. What are, from Robbins' chapter or your own reflection, some things to watch out for?

13) Envision yourself as a youth pastor; your church has given you the responsibility to come up with 5-10 guidelines that will help you and your staff avoid sexual misconduct. What would you include on this list?

Ideas For a Major Project or Paper

1) Find five contemporary Christian songs (preferably with music videos if possible) that deal with the five danger areas that Robbins refers to in this chapter. (One song per danger area, if possible.) Explain how the lyrics connect to the danger area. If you can't find a contemporary Christian song, try a hymn. Failing that, try a secular song.

2) Some excellent resources are included in and around footnote 54. Obtain these books: *In the Name of Jesus*, *The Unnecessary Partner*, and *Courage and Calling*. With your ministry-seeking peers who are not in this class in mind, write a substantial book review for each book.

3) Do a major research project on the subject of sexual misconduct in youth ministry. Consider consulting *The Youth Minister's Survival Guide* (Kageler), *Better Safe than Sued* (Crabtree), and *Feeding Your Forgotten Soul* (Borthwick). *Youthworker Journal* has good material on this as well. You will find ample policy statements and news stories through a google.com search. Be sure to include in your paper something like "Ways to Avoid."

Unit 2:
Understanding the Terrain

CHAPTER 5

CHANGING PACES:
ADVENTURES IN THE "LAND OF THERE BUT NOT THERE"

WARM UP

Think about your own upbringing. When, if ever, did your parents begin to treat you as something more than just a child? In what ways have they supported, encouraged, or fostered your own transition from childhood to adulthood? In what ways have they denied or hindered the process?

CASE STUDIES

Case 12

One of my daughters was on a community track team, the Rain City Flyers, when she was in fifth grade. She enjoyed being with her friends and getting to go to different parks for track meets. She wasn't good at jumping or throwing things, so about all she could do was run. There were only two problems with this. First, she didn't like to train, that is, actually practice running. Second, if she did practice and tried to run fast, she'd vomit, or at least feel like vomiting. But hey, she wasn't trying for the Olympics or a university track scholarship. She just liked being outside, with friends, and going to McDonald's on the way home.

As a parent I actually enjoyed going to her track meets. She never even came close to winning, but she participated and that was the fun. And I liked being outside, too.

It was very interesting to watch other parents watch their own kids, as well as to see how kids managed the "pressure" of a community track meet.

One time the first race, a 50-yard dash, was for the really little kids. I suppose these boys were only five or six. About 10 of them lined up, the "gun" sounded, and they were off! Arms flailing, chests heaving, these boys were in a dash for their lives. Parents and team members yelled encouragement. One boy, with about 10 yards to go, was in first place by a couple of feet. But just before the finish line, number two passed him and crossed first. The place erupted in cheers of support for all 10 runners. There was one problem, however. The boy who thought he was going to finish first and instead finished second stopped as soon as he crossed the finish line. He squinted his eyes and then put both hands flat against the side of his head and started to cry. This was not a quiet, private, sobbing. These were deep wails of anguish and disappointment. The crowd grew silent; we all just sat or stood there transfixed by the very public agony of that five-year-old. Finally, after about 10 or 15 seconds, an adult, I assume his mother, ran to him and escorted him off the track.

I think of this boy from time to time at the middle school youth group where I volunteer my time. We were outside, playing a team game that involves the team that is "up" running in pairs the length of the basketball court while the team that is "out in the field" is lined up on both long court sidelines, trying to hit the two runners with one of two soft playground balls. Nick was a new sixth grader. Like all new sixth graders just coming into the strange and wonderful world of middle school, he was excited, nervous, and wanted to be the epitome of "coolness."

Nick was eleven years old but looked about eight or nine. His team was up. While running as fast as he could, he got smacked on the side of the face with a hard-thrown ball. He stopped, put his hand flat to the sides of his face, and cried. The older (seventh and eighth grade) kids looked at him in disgust. There is an unwritten rule in middle school, it seems: don't cry no matter how hard it hurts. Nick was clueless about this rule and didn't stop crying until one of the staff took him inside and got some ice on his very red face.

I thought of the track-meet-crying-five-year-old boy another time. I was playing "keep away" with the kids outside when a mother came up to me. "Could you come inside?" she asked. "This is Evan's first night here. He's going into sixth grade but he skipped a year in school so he's really only 10. He's crying on the couch in there and he's very afraid." I followed her inside, and wow, this kid was small. Sure enough, he was trying to hold back the tears, but not very successfully.

Occasionally I manage to say the right thing to a kid, and that night I think I did. After introductions, while his mother watched, I sat next to him on the couch and put my hand on his shoulder. "Evan, I know that it looks like everyone out there has been friends for years, but just a few weeks ago many of them were brand-new too. I want you to know it is very normal to be scared in a new situation like this. I guarantee that many of those outside were just as scared and nervous as you seem to be now. It's okay! Would you be willing to try an experiment?"

Evan nodded apprehensively.

"Promise me you'll come to youth group three weeks in a row. By then you'll have friends, and it will be a lot more fun than it seems now. Would you do that for me?"

He looked up at me with his eyes still full of tears, but with hope. I could barely hear what he said, but I know his lips moved, and I'm pretty sure he said, "Okay."

Anyway, I took it for an okay and said then, "Good, let's go meet some of the guys." I glanced at his mom as Evan and I walked out of the room. Her eyes were full of tears by now, but hopeful ones.

As I led Evan out to the court to introduce him, I mentally prayed, "Oh God, may no one here tonight look at Evan and call him a dumb punk." (No one did.) Evan had a great time that night and in three weeks he did have friends and couldn't stop talking, according to his mom, about how "cool" the group was. Whew!

—L.K.

Case 13

As a youth pastor one of my favorite things has always been working with leadership kids. They've been called different things at different churches, like youth council, the cabinet, leadership team, and so on. But their functions have all been the same. I expect these leadership kids to be growing in Christ, to be as committed to the group as they would be committed to a school sports team, and always to be looking for ways to include peripheral or new youth into the ministry. We have a high level of accountability and meet twice monthly. The last thing we do is put the folding chairs in a circle, kneel facing the center of the circle, and pray for the ministry itself. I've found that this regular act of kneeling and praying with students changes their hearts more than any amount of training. Pretty soon they start coming to group stuff as givers, not takers. Well, at least it works this way in theory. For another take on this turn to Case Study 33.

It was after a normal Wednesday night meeting. Most of the senior highs had gone home and I was cleaning up the refreshment table when I saw Pam, a 12th-grader and one of my most discipled, committed leadership girls, talking with Ashley. Ashley was a new and very physically attractive freshman whose family had just started to attend our church. I only caught the tail end of their conversation when Pam said, "So Ashley, you see, we really don't want or need you here!"

I looked up to see Ashley look at Pam with hate-filled eyes. She wheeled around and stormed out the door. Pam left by another exit, without glancing at me or acknowledging my presence. I had a little trouble getting to sleep that night.

What happened after that? Ashley came back, to Sunday School, youth group, and all our student ministry events. She was a vivacious new presence. Guys who were formerly Pam's admirers started to flock around Ashley. Pam was one unhappy camper, and she never showed regard for Ashley, other than contempt. The weather in our ministry for the remaining few months of that school year turned rather chilly. Things didn't warm up again until Pam graduated that June and was out of the group.

—L.K.

Reflections on Cases 12 and 13

1) How do the boys in case 12 illustrate Robbins' notion of "there but not there"?

2) What are your own memories of anticipation or dread about entering middle school or high school? If you were in a church or parachurch youth group, was it a place of safety, or stress, or both? How?

3) Robbins speaks of adolescence as revealing things about both biology and sociology. Evaluate both of these cases using conceptualizations from both subject areas.

4) Sociology, boiled down to a single notion, is about how people are in groups. In what ways do you think these cases reveal group expectations, group norms, and group dynamics?

FOR FURTHER DISCUSSION:

Thinking About Adolescence

5) Share examples from your own life that illustrate adolescence as "the perfect storm" or "a mighty river."

6) What are some of the major markers of progress into and through adolescence you are familiar with? (For example, your first part-time job.)

7) Are you familiar with markers of other cultures? How are they different or better defined than your own?

8) Robbins says Jesus was an adolescent. Prepare, with some others in the class, a presentation in skit form of some of the issues Jesus may have faced as "Son of God, Teenager."

9) Go to the mall or a teen hang-out of your choice. Sit for an hour and watch kids. Come back with reflections on adolescence related to biology and sociology.

Ideas for a major project or paper

1) Compare the lyrics of the top five hit singles young people are listening to today. Evaluate these songs as examples of "the perfect storm" or "a mighty river." Here are two suggestions as to how to gain the song lyrics. If you have regular access to middle school or senior high youths, ask them for this information and they will probably be happy to get you the songs and the lyrics. Or, get the information the old-fashioned way: research: Go to Billboard.com and under Charts choose Singles and Tracks. You'll have several categories to choose from, such as the Billboard Hot 100, Hot R&B/Hip Hop, Modern Rock, Hot Latin, and so on. Select a category and get the top five from the list. Then go to lyrics.com (or any other web-based lyrics site) to obtain the lyrics.

2) Obtain a recent copy of *Seventeen* magazine or other similar youth-oriented magazine. Read it from cover to cover, including all the advertisements. Write a paper or prepare a presentation that illustrates the nature of adolescence in the terms and concepts used in the chapter.

3) Do a study comparing the "rites of passage" of at least five different cultures.

CHAPTER 6

CONVERGING CURRENTS:
EXPLORING ADOLESCENT DEVELOPMENT

WARM UP

Recall a time in your very early adolescence when you did something or thought something that was, now that you think of it, really immature.

CASE STUDIES

Case 14, part one

I was having one of those nights with our middle school group where everything went right. Well, almost everything. Attendance was good, and the games went well. The kids (about 40 of them, 11-to 13-years-old) participated with enthusiasm and did not adopt an "I'm too cool for this" attitude. They sat quietly when I was giving the Bible study and many hands shot up when I asked discussion questions. (I told you it was a good night!) My theme was unity and being kind to one another. The main point was, just like the early church, our group was very diverse, yet it could be a safe place. Heads were nodding. It was one of those times when, had it been a camp situation, we would have joined hands around the campfire and sung "Kumbaya" or an Amy Grant classic, with faces and hearts aglow.

When we closed in prayer, over half the kids prayed out loud, offering thanksgiving to God for our group or praying that we would be kind, have unity, and so on. You may be thinking this story is too good to be true, but believe me, it was one of those nights where things went right. Right, that is, until just after the last "amen."

On my left side were the guys. They often tried to act tough, macho, and oh-so-cool. The girls were on my right. Two seconds after I said "amen" and we were all just enjoying the moment, Troy yelled, "Hey Jenny, you're fat and ugly!" He rolled over in laughter and was joined by most of the other guys in uproarious delight at such a well-timed insult. Jenny stood, burst into tears, and ran from the room.

The rest of the group quickly dispersed as parents arrived to pick up their kids. It didn't take a Ph.D. to speculate what would be reported to parents on the way home.

—L.K. (Adapted from *How to Expand Your Youth Ministry*)

Reflections on Case 14

1) If this had happened to you, which do you feel would have been the best course of action?

(Option for instructors: write five columns on the board, one through five. Have your students come to the board *en masse* and place a mark under the number that represents their selection from the choices below.)

Response 1: Confront Troy, banish him from the group for a month as discipline.

Response 2: Call a parent meeting to go over acceptable behavior standards in youth group meetings.

Response 3: Call the pastor and elders to report the incident; perhaps then seek a meeting with Troy and his parents to agree on appropriate discipline.

Response 4: Fill in the blank!

Response 5: Resign your position, seek a career with Home Depot or Starbucks.

2) What response did you choose? Why?

Case 14, part two

If you're wondering, here's what I did with Troy: I caught up with him in the parking lot and said, "Troy, I was a little confused by what you did in there. Weren't you one of the people who thanked God for the wonderful feeling and unity we have in this group?"

Troy replied, "She's my sister, I can say what I want."

"Well, Troy," I said, "I know you'll feel differently about what you did tonight eventually." He turned and got into the car that was waiting to take him and Jenny home.

I didn't worry about the incident or do anything to follow up. I knew Troy was pre-formal operations (Piaget, see Robbins page 198). I call it pre-cerebral upgrade. I knew that when Troy got his cerebral upgrade it would finally occur to him that the Christian faith actually should apply at home and at school, not just in youth group on Wednesday nights. By the time a year had passed and Troy was in ninth grade, he had had his upgrade and was very much a Christian who evidenced the fruit of the Spirit at home with his sister, and everywhere.

Case 15

The retreat was the second one I had been on with these teens. The camp is a beautiful place, right on the lake; even the dorms are great. Months before the retreat the teens were talking about how excited they were to go. They had a great time last year and were looking forward to this year's retreat.

As we got to the retreat center, the kids were bursting with excitement and acting like little kids who have had too much candy (which they had!). We got our room assignments and settled in. I called a meeting to go over the schedule of events throughout the weekend and to bring order back to the group. The teens listened and they calmed down for our first big group session, where we sat and listened to the speaker.

Afterwards the teens had free time and then lights out. That first night the free time was only a half-hour long. Everything seemed too quiet. The girls were settling down in their room, and so were the boys, or so I thought.

As I walked into the boys' room I noticed two of my senior high guys jumping down from their bunk beds. I looked up. There were two huge holes in the ceiling!

Let me tell you a little about these two guys that put the two huge holes in the ceiling. These are guys that any father would want their daughters to marry. They are well-rounded and, most importantly, love the Lord with all their hearts. And to top it off, they are my senior high teen leaders!

So back to the holes. As they were in their room, just chillin,' they heard loud noises from the room above them. So they decided to get on the top bunk, and with their backs against the mattress, used their feet to bang back. The people above them heard them and banged back; they did this for awhile. The thing is, my two guys didn't know that when you put too much force on sheet rock, it breaks! And so they put their feet right through the ceiling, leaving two huge holes.

—Josh

Case 16

Ah, youth group night, a night that all youth pastors look forward to. They get to see their flock of teenagers, they get to play crazy games, and they get to act like teens again.

The teens were looking forward to this particular night. It was the foosball tournament night. Foosball is huge in our youth group; they love the game and have become very good at it. I set up the youth room to look like a tournament with the foosball table in the middle of the room under a 600-watt light.

The games were intense, as we all wanted the bragging rights to say we were the best foosball players. At half-time we took a break. I had them all sit down and we went over some announcements and a discussion on "how are things going in your life." They were all listening to the announcements, because a new month was coming with new events to look forward to.

Then we got right back to foosball. As the final game was going on, the game that decided the winners, I heard one of the girls say, "Is anyone here Mexican?" She looked around the room, saw no Mexicans, and then said, "Good, because I think they should go back to Mexico!"

You could have heard a pin drop. The teens were thinking, "Did she really just say what I think she said?" The girl noticed that people were looking at her funny and said, "Well, it's true, they should." Half of the teens are from ethnic backgrounds other than white, and I can't imagine what they were thinking. We even had an Asian girl come to youth group because her friend, also Asian, told her it was a fun, safe place to hang out!

One of my adult leaders went on to correct the teen who had made the comment. But you have to wonder, why did she feel the need to test her audience in that way? Why couldn't she just keep her mouth shut?

—Josh

Case 17

Marcus: In middle school ministry I deal with pre-cerebral upgrade boys all the time. Marcus was in eighth grade, and by the middle of that year he was almost 6 feet tall and weighed nearly 200 pounds. Some of the sixth graders in the group were only chest height to him and far less than half his weight. Anyway, Marcus loved to hog a whole couch to himself when we came in from playing group games outside. He would run into the youth room, jump over the back of a couch, and spread himself out to take all three or four seats. If there was another kid already on the couch, Marcus just took one of his size-12 feet and shoved the kid until the couch was his alone.

Marcus had a good side, however. I could see that during the Bible study time he was listening some of the time. He even occasionally made a comment or asked a question that showed some promise of cerebral activity.

One evening I purposely ran in from outside next to Marcus, jumped over the back of the couch, and plopped down next to him.

"Hey, Marcus, got a question for you."

"What's up?"

"How old do you think you'll be when you stop hogging the couch all to yourself?"

"What do you mean?" He looked at me with eyes wide.

"What I mean is, when you get into the high school group next year you'll probably observe that no one behaves the way you do when it comes to couch sitting. So, I was just curious, what year in high school do you think you might be when you are actually polite to people and even a little bit considerate?"

Marcus stared at me. "I dunno."

He never hogged the couch again.

Brian. Brian had a gift for verbal torture. He was a seventh grader and exceedingly hyperactive. One of his main activities before and after youth group was to tease, ridicule, and humiliate Missy, a little sixth-grade girl who was home-schooled. Brian projected the image of cool, urbane, hip, popular, and worldly-wise. He took every opportunity he could to help Missy know she was the absolute opposite. I had to hand it to Missy—she seemed generally unfazed by this negative attention. She was a deeply Christian girl (for a sixth grader, anyway) and although I'm sure she would rather not have been faced with Brian's onslaughts each week, nevertheless she came faithfully, week after week.

The youth pastor had addressed the group generally about how we treat each other, but Brian either didn't listen or didn't care. I did notice, though, that on rare occasions in Bible study, Brian actually had something insightful to say, giving us glimpses of what I hoped would emerge as the mature Christian Brian. I pictured him like someone with one foot on the dock and one foot on the rowboat.

On a night in which Brian's verbal abuse of Missy had risen to new heights, I pulled him aside physically—not in anger, but in a way that made it clear he was to come with me.

"Brian, I'm going to give you some feedback. I know you are not asking for any, but I'm going to give you some feedback anyway."

He stared off into space, avoiding my eyes.

"If I was from another planet and was visiting the earth for the very first time and was sitting here in this last half hour, I would have concluded that it was your sole purpose as a human being to torture Missy. I would have guessed that this is all you have had on your mind all day, and that tonight, now that you two are in the same place, you are unleashing all the negative things you've been planning against her."

He continued to stare away.

"So I guess I'm a little confused. In Bible study sometimes you seem to say that you are a Christian and believe the Bible and stuff. Yet out here, you are clearly trying to make Missy not only miserable here, but miserable that she was ever born in the first place. So, what gives? Help me understand."

He just ran off to join his friends.

However, Brian did not come near Missy the rest of the evening, or the next week either. As far as I observed and know from others, Brian completely ceased his rotten treatment of this sixth-grade home-schooled girl, who moved away at the end of the school year.

—L.K.

Reflections on Cases 14-17

3) How might Piaget view the actions of the kids in these cases? Support your position.

4) Obviously, to be able to handle early adolescent immaturity from week to week, some things have to be true of youth workers. What must be true of you to be with the Troys, Brians, and Marcuses of youth ministry?

5) The author of cases 14 and 17 used a very soft approach to these misbehaving guys, based on his understanding of Piaget and cognitive development. Reflect on your own misbehavior or the misbehavior of others in early adolescence. What "discipline" approach did your teachers or youth leaders use on you or the ones you know? Did it work? Why or why not?

6) Prepare a role play in which the parents of Troy, Marcus, and Brian will each, in turn come to you as a counselor. These parents are near nervous breakdowns over the behavior of their kids. What counsel will you give? Explain Piaget to each in terms that are specific to each boys' issues.

7) The author of case 17 was consciously trying to help Brian and Marcus get to a higher stage of cognitive development. Upon reflection, can you think of other teachers or leaders who you now realize were trying to do the same thing? What did they do? Did it work?

Ideas for a major project or paper

1) Find three to five television or movie clips that illustrate pre-formal operations and formal operations behavior in adolescents. The clips themselves should be one to five minutes in length. (Make a copy for your professor to keep so that he or she can use it the next time this subject is taught!) Be prepared to present in class.

2) Extensively interview either five of your friends or five youth who are age 17 or 18. Document their own transitions from pre-cerebral upgrade to the cerebral upgrade stage.

CHAPTER 7

EXPLORING THE INNER PASSAGES OF ADOLESCENCE: MORAL CHOICES AND EMERGING IDENTITY

WARM UP

Share with the class a time in your life when you were not sure who you were. Robbins' chapter speaks of Erickson and identity confusion. Can you recall a time when this was true for you?

CASE STUDIES

Case 18

It was only 15 minutes before our middle school youth group meeting would start. I was in the youth center, putting the finishing touches on the place, like straightening couch cushions, making sure the music was at just the right level and that the pool table wasn't missing the eight ball...again.

Tonight, Tim was one of the first kids to show up. For the two minutes of relative quiet before the storm, I enjoyed catching up with Tim about school, friends, family, et cetera. He seemed to really be opening up. That is, until Jeff arrived. Just the sight of Jeff in the doorway sent Tim quickly and nearly unnoticeably scurrying for cover. Tim knew all too well that Jeff derived great pleasure out of their weekly bullying sessions. Tim is home-schooled, uncoordinated, and short. Jeff is a full-grown 13-year-old who is athletic and slick. It wasn't long before my back was turned and those nicely straightened couch cushions become weapons used on Tim. And it was only a matter of time before other guys entered the room, and knowing full well their place in the "pecking order," would give and receive their fair share of jabbing and name calling. Words like "idio" and "gay" were more commonly heard than words like "excellent" or "God."

The rest of the kids trickled in until the place was buzzing with adrenaline. I loved to see them come and they all loved being there—well, almost all of them. The kids made their way around the youth center and each other, taking their places with their friends. It was so predictable who would gravitate to what group. Like a well-organized closet, with a place for everything and everything in its place, the sign above the youth center door could have read, "A place for every kid and every kid in his place"—and how they enjoyed putting each other in their place.

I stepped in, trying to subdue the savages who had converged on Tim. But I knew that Tim didn't want to be defended, he just wanted to be left alone. The other guys did lay off Tim, but it was only a few minutes before another opportunity arose to bring him down. After a few minutes, we got into our group games and lesson time, but I could tell that Tim was uneasy the whole time. At the end of the night I knew that once again, damage control would have to be done, and Tim would once again need to be persuaded to return next week.

—Jerry

Case 19

I was nervous during the drive home that Wednesday afternoon. On Wednesday nights I met with my discipleship girls. I really enjoyed my times with them. They were high school cheerleaders who were hungry for God and usually asked more questions than I could handle.

I had heard from another youth worker in my parachurch organization that these girls had been drinking heavily at a party. Her source was a student who knew these girls and attended their school. I wasn't sure how much was true, but I knew that either way I would have to confront the issue some time soon. They were part of the popular crowd, and I knew there was an image they had to maintain. My prayer was that they would have enough courage and trust in me to talk about it.

That night I was meeting with Jocelyn and Carla. I picked the girls up as usual, and the Bible study went as planned. As soon as our closing prayer ended, they both looked up and smiled. Carla turned to Jocelyn and asked her, "Wait, don't you want to tell her about what happened the other night?" Jocelyn answered with an enthusiastic "Oh yeah, yeah." The girls proceeded to tell me about the party. At this point I knew I would get the real story. I was relieved they brought up the subject.

The party was thrown by one of the other cheerleaders. The basketball team had lost an important game so there was a lot of disappointment floating through the air (a good excuse to get drunk). There wasn't supposed to be any alcohol, and the girl hosting the party said it herself. Then a few of the real popular guys arrived, bringing booze. In the blink of an eye, everyone was helping themselves to free drinks.

Almost everyone was getting drunk, including one of the other Christian girls on the cheerleading team. Carla and Jocelyn felt the heat of the pressure. They were the oddballs for not drinking, but they had their reasons for abstaining.

Jocelyn respected her older sister who was in college. She could recall her sister's disapproval of high school age students getting drunk. Her sister thought that kids like that were losers with nothing better to do. Jocelyn also remembered her own drinking phase. She remembered the shame that she felt when her sister had found out about it. Jocelyn did not want to face her sister and feel that self-reproach again.

Carla felt the pressure, but she was dead-set on not drinking. In fact, she recruited a "no drinking" partner at the beginning of the party. Only the partner turned shallow when the waves of pressure flooded in. At the party Carla watched many make fools of themselves. At one point someone made a dare for someone else to strip. Their friend got on the table and began loosening her belt. It was a good thing that Carla and Jocelyn were sober and had the sense to stop her. Carla was reminded of the loss of respect that accompanies decisions like that. Carla also remembered her mother's struggle with alcoholism. To Carla, one night of drinking was not worth the regret she knew she might face.

So that was it: I got the whole story from the girls themselves. Carla mentioned how proud she was to get up the next day and know she had made the right decision. The girls asked me questions about alternatives to drinking and what they should do at their prom. That night I was thankful that God allowed me to witness the work he was doing in their lives.

—Sarah

Case 20

"You know, I've been coming to youth group for a while, but it's just in these past few weeks that I think I'm really getting it. Like, Jesus really died for me and it's not about how good I am or anything, it's all about Jesus and me trusting him, and it's so cool! God is way cool!"

If I could have jumped up and down while I was driving my car and listening to this student, I would have! These words were spoken by Carrie, a high school student who had been invited to an outreach by her friends in our youth ministry and had since become actively involved with us. No greater joy than a young person making a commitment to Christ!

As I continued to drive that warm spring evening, silently praising God for Carrie's testimony, I verbally encouraged her commitment. I dropped her off, told her I would continue to pray for her, and drove home—on a youth worker's cloud nine! I began to plan ways to help Carrie grow in her new faith, along with a few other students who had recently trusted Christ.

Carrie seemed like a unique individual—highly intelligent, outspoken, wickedly funny, and unafraid to go "against the flow." She was artistic, musical, and known for making fashion statements wherever she went (and not in the Gap and Abercrombie sense)! Everything about Carrie proclaimed that she wasn't a crowd-follower; she was her own individual. Exactly who that individual was, I'm not sure if she knew herself; but she was unafraid to "try on" different things that would set her apart from the crowd.

Carrie's family weren't churchgoers, but her mom and younger sister soon started attending our church with Carrie, much to our joy. As for Carrie herself, she continued to grow in her knowledge of Scripture, formed fast friendships with strong Christian students in our youth group, and took every opportunity to be involved in ministry.

I delighted in Carrie's unique personality and her commitment, and I worked hard to help her solidify her relationship with Christ. But while everything looked great on the surface, I admit I had a few concerns—a big one being that Carrie's motivation for being involved in the youth ministry at all seemed to be heavily influenced by her friendships with other students, including a guy student leader whom she "greatly admired." Wanting to give Carrie the benefit of the doubt, I reasoned that many students could initially be drawn to Christ because of relationships, but would eventually find their relationship with Christ to be much deeper and unfading.

Looking back, perhaps I should have seen more warning signs than I did. We began to give Carrie some responsibilities in the ministry, which she was eager to accept. But as the new school year started that fall, things began to "come up," leading her to be late to meetings or miss them altogether. Her student partners in leadership grew frustrated because she seemed disinterested in leading anymore. Whenever I would question her about it, she would tell me that things were fine; she was just very busy. Oh, and there was also a new guy friend on the scene, one who was no doubt a fine person but nonetheless not a believer and not involved in our youth ministry—and eventually pulled Carrie in a different direction. Over the course of another year, she faded out of the youth ministry and out of church (along with her family) altogether.

When it came down to it, I'm afraid that being committed to Christ meant more change than Carrie had bargained for. Only God knows the sincerity of her heart, but I wonder if her initial commitment was in some ways just another new thing to "try on," as she had tried on so many things before. I still pray that Carrie will discover again the relationship with Christ that she set aside in favor of better options, and realize that only in surrendering her life to him will she find the true individuality God created for her.

—Faith

Case 21

One of the most amazing things to me about being a paid youth pastor is that I actually get paid to do the things I enjoy doing, like skiing and backpacking. In one church I served we skied a lot. In a typical season we would go skiing for a full day twice, go night skiing once, have a one-night retreat for night skiing once, and have a weekend retreat which included two days of skiing.

One tradition we had was going skiing on Presidents' Day Monday. We'd gather at the church at 6 a.m. and arrive at the mountain around 8 a.m. We purchased lift tickets and were among the first up the slopes when the mountain officially opened at 8:30 a.m. On this particular Presidents' Day, the church bus was full and everyone was excited about the day ahead. Robbie, one of the core senior highers on our leadership team, seemed especially happy and outgoing that day. Uncharacteristically, he sat near the back of the bus, and on the slopes I hardly saw him all day.

At the end of the day when we were boarding the bus to come back home, Vanessa, also a senior high leadership team member, whispered to me, "Robbie's acting a little strange."

I later learned that "a little strange" was an understatement for Robbie's behavior. He swore frequently that day, including multiple uses of the f-word with a variety of endings and combinations. He was verbally abusive to some on the trip. He even urinated in a sink in a public restroom crowded with not only our kids but also others.

The following Sunday Robbie took his normal place as small group leader in Sunday school and he was his normal self. On the following Wednesday at youth group he again was his normal, "spiritual" self, making various helpful contributions to the Bible study discussion and freely contributing prayers when it came time for conversational prayer at the end. During refreshments he actively sought out "loners" as he usually did, helping people feel welcome.

Vanessa commented to me as she went out the door that night, "Robbie's normal again, thank God."

I didn't confront Robbie or even bring up his ski-day behavior. As I told Vanessa, I just figured "he tried on a different persona. Guess he didn't like it. Thank God."

—L.K.

Case 22, part one

My first inkling that something had gone wrong was during the beginning of the worship service. My family and I were at our church family weekend retreat. There were also around 40 teenagers there, mostly from church families as well. The theory of the church family retreat was that there would be a lot of unstructured time so families could be together. On this, the second day, I was already realizing that the theory was working out for families with small children, but that the teenagers were definitely not hanging out with their parents. They were hanging out with other teens, and there wasn't much for them to do. I remember thinking, "Could be trouble," but I wasn't in charge, so I tried not to worry.

I was called out of the worship service when a friend came up behind me with the words, "Len, you'd better go see the rec building."

The recreation building had a nice pool table and two ping-pong tables. When I entered the room my heart sank. The walls were riddled with either holes or indentations the size of pool balls. I was then informed that most of the guys had decided it would be cool to see who could throw a pool ball completely through a nicely finished, sheet-rock wall. In other words, they had absolutely destroyed the place. I guessed I was looking at thousands of dollars worth of damage.

—L.K.

Reflections on Cases 18-22

1) These cases are full of issues raised in Robbins' text. What examples of moral development (or lack thereof) do you find? If you were the youth pastor around these cases, how would you have responded and why?

2) There are examples of identity confusion in the cases as well. Specifically, how do you see identity confusion here?

3) From what you read in the chapter regarding attachment theory, how would you guess it might connect to the concept of identity confusion?

4) You have probably gathered from the number and variety of cases presented here that it is the normal experience of youth workers to be with kids who are in the various stages described in the chapter. Also in the cases you see that youths in some of these stages make ministry a challenge. Go back through Robbins' chapter and glean at least one insight from each section that you'll want to be sure to remember as you anticipate working with adolescents in the future.

Case 22, part two

I turned right around and went back to the worship center. I walked down the center aisle, up to the front (with all 200 or so people now wondering what the heck I was doing) and stopped the service. I took the microphone, and in as calm a voice as possible said, "I need every male junior or senior higher to come with me immediately, right now."

I marched back down the aisle, pausing at the rows that contained male youth, and made it clear I was expecting them to follow.

The 20 or so guys and I then sat down on the floor in the rec center. I began, still trying very hard to control my rage, "I'm a little confused. I need to understand what happened here."

Eventually the whole story came out. (Pistol whipping and electric shock therapy helped. Just kidding!) I had the boys wait there; I went to nab the fathers after the service to bring them into the rec room. Then I walked out of the room, now full of men and boys, with these words: "You have to figure this out."

Over the next several Saturdays the boys and their fathers came back. They stripped the whole room down to the studs, replaced the sheet rock, and finally painted the whole room. The camp was satisfied that the room had been restored completely.

FOR FURTHER DISCUSSION:

Kohlberg Revisited

Though not brought out in Robbins' chapter, Kohlberg speculates that it is possible to help kids get from one moral stage of development to another. He says,

> The more social settings encourage role taking, voluntary participation, communication, and decision making, the more the individual confronted with these settings will advance to higher stages of moral consciousness.

5) A well-developed youth ministry is an almost perfect means to achieve higher moral development in Kohlberg's framework. List at least five features of a normal youth group that Kohlberg would applaud as helpful for moral development.

For a Major Paper or Project

1) Find at least five movie clips that illustrate some of the concepts in Robbins's text. Be prepared to share in class a clear explanation of their theoretical linkages to the conceptualizations in the text. (If possible, make a copy of your presentation for your professor to use the next time he or she teaches this subject.)

2) Gather a few of your friends and come up with your own personal case studies illustrating the major concepts in the text. Write them up as case studies, but also prepare to present them as role plays to the class for their own analysis. Help your classmates identify the issues of moral development, attachment, or identity confusion you are illustrating.

3) If you feel a little overwhelmed and even intimidated by the thought of dealing with teen misbehavior, good! It requires a closeness to God and reliance on godly wisdom that goes much deeper than many think.

   a) Interview five full-time youth pastors to find out how they handle some of the things that the case studies in this chapter bring up. Hear their stories and find out what they did, for better or worse.

   b) Go back though chapter five, six, and seven. Picture yourself now as a youth pastor in charge or training your own volunteer youth staff. You want them to have helpful insights about adolescents…what is normal and how to deal with adolescent behavior. Prepare a 30-60 minute seminar, in outline form, showing what you would cover in such a training session. Make your notes complete enough so you could actually use it in a real life situation.

CHAPTER 8

READING THE WATER:
THINKING ABOUT CULTURE

WARM UP

Have some fun thinking about yourself as a 13- or 14-year-old. What were some popular slang phrases or words? Do you recall an absolute favorite song or singer or band that you and your friends enjoyed? Are these words, songs, and bands still as popular now?

CASE STUDIES

Case 23

If there is a need to be met and you can meet it, you do so. The need that was obvious to me was a place for kids in our community to skateboard and inline skate. This activity was simply not allowed in our town on any public property. So, the church leadership supported the youth ministry as it built a large halfpipe skate ramp to meet this need. Teens from the community worked together to get plywood at a discount price from a local lumberyard. I worked with them to pick up the large amounts of lumber and construct the ramp on the youth center property. It was a large investment of time and energy. We made sure our insurance "ducks" were in a row. Everything was set, and the old saying definitely rang true: "If you build it, they will come."

With a consistent daily crowd of 40 to 50 teens, it became clear that an adult leadership presence was needed. Not merely for policing or deterring vandalism (which did occur), but more importantly, to build bridges of friendship with these skaters. As I soon learned in that world, you better skate or get out of the way. I learned that nobody came to talk to me. They came because we offered an open paved area, a grind rail, a launch ramp, and a halfpipe. So, if I wasn't going to be a part of any of those activities, I simply wasn't going to get a chance to talk to anybody about anything.

I used to skateboard. It was back in the day when skateboards had a nose and a tail. It was when skaters were nothing more than surfers when the waves went flat. All these kick-flips, ollies, nollies, fakies, pop-shove-its, and all the other lingo was utter newness to me. But I bought a board, mooched some trucks and wheels, and hit the asphalt. Little by little, I found that the door of communication and friendship was beginning to unlock. The more I skated, the more I practiced, the more I found that kids were open to the "old guy with the new board." It was embarrassing to fall, but in the world of skateboarding, it's not the fall, but the rebound that counts. So I got up again and again and again. And found that the kids' resentment of my presence turned to tolerance and then enjoyment. Did we still have halfpipe break-ins in the middle of the night? Sure. Did we still seek to curb the profanity and smoking? Yes, we did. But through it all, I found that no subculture is impenetrable. Not even the strange and wonderful world of skaters.

—Jerry

Case 24

When I heard the news early that Sunday morning, it did not full register in my mind. I did not realize that they were talking about her or the severity of the situation. However, the flood of phone calls and tears quickly changed my state of mind. This was actually happening. It was real.

On a Sunday in August the church received the awful news that one of our students had been in a horrible car accident. Diana was a beautiful high school senior who could light up a room with her personality and smile. She was the star soccer player in the county, a member of the drama club, and part of an elite a cappella group. She was one of those girls that every boy was in love with. Spiritually, she was top-notch. You could build an incredible, vital youth ministry around her.

The student ministry had just returned from a mission trip to Mexico. There were a total of 86 people on the trip, but the one who was determined to change her world for Christ was Diana. The theme of the trip was "Use your life to change a life," and she desired to accomplish that. She had made a goal of telling all of her friends about the trip with the hope of bringing them with her to Mexico.

I had the task of explaining to our students that she had been in a terrible head-on car accident and that it did not look good, but we needed to pray. (My boss, the director of student ministries, was on vacation.) We prayed diligently through both worship services. After church a few of us went to get some lunch. When we returned to the church we became a part of something unexpected. When I got out of the car, I saw about 20 students outside of church sitting on the curbs and sobbing. Quickly the 20 turned into 50 and then 100, and eventually around 200-plus students and parents arrived at the church. They were seeking answers, wondering what had happened and how could this have happened. I was the only pastor available, along with a couple of adults present. I decided to invite everyone into our chapel. I explained what I knew had happened and the situation. I led the students in a quick prayer and encouraged them to break up into smaller groups to pray and discuss what they were feeling. Out of more than 200 who were at the church that Sunday afternoon, about 75 percent of them had never stepped inside our church before this day.

We stayed at the church for hours that day, praying with those who wanted to, talking with those who needed to talk, and providing refreshments. Even as I look back upon the situation, it is still a blur. The long day came to an end when our senior executive pastor came back from the hospital with the news that the doctors were going to take Diana off life support. The student were angry, confused, and drained. We prayed for them and encouraged them to spend time with their families.

On the way home, my wife reminded me that this day, August 25, was the one-month anniversary of my being in full-time youth ministry. I thought to myself, "Wow! What a first month! A mission trip to Mexico, a K-8th grade VBS program with more than 1,000 people, and now this. I hope not everyone's first month of ministry is like this."

—Ryan

Case 25

I've been in youth ministry for over three decades, so I've had lots of time to make mistakes when it comes to understanding and interacting with youth culture and group norms.

In my first church I tried to impose what I felt comprised a "comfortable environment" on a group of kids who were used to something else. It was stupid, now that I think about it, but I felt strongly that kids would be more comfortable sitting on a carpeted floor during their meetings than they would on wood and metal chairs. The first several meetings I insisted that they leave the chairs aside and join me on the floor when it came to settle down in our meetings. The only problem was, no one did. It was really weird with me sitting on the floor, looking up at them sitting around me in chairs. It didn't take me many weeks to jettison that idea!

I made another mistake when it came to youth culture at my second church. I knew kids did not want or expect me to dress just like them, but I should at least be somewhere in the ballpark of acceptability. In summer all the kids wore shorts to youth group, as did I. Imagine how I felt when during a Bible study, I was mid-sentence when it hit me: I was the only male in the room wearing socks. I managed to complete the evening, but I could just imagine my kids laughing about how stupid I looked with my nice white socks. Sigh.

At my third church (on the East Coast, now, instead of the West Coast) I was confused as to why I was having such trouble getting pizza for the pizza party. We were going to need about seven extra-large pizzas, so I thought I'd get two plain and five with the Canadian bacon and pineapple combination. Place after place I called didn't carry the latter. Finally I found a place and ordered my pizzas. That night at youth group I almost had a revolution on my hands. Most of the kids wouldn't touch the non-plain pizzas. I learned that night that Canadian bacon and pineapple is most definitely a West Coast favorite. On the East Coast it's called Hawaiian, and almost no one eats it.

Here's another miscue. A few weeks later a family invited my family over for pie after church. I was wondering what it would be—apple, blueberry, peach, or maybe my favorite, pecan. I tried to conceal my disappointment when they hauled out pizza. It was plain cheese, thin crust, and very greasy. They laughed and laughed when I eventually mentioned the misunderstanding about the word "pie." They also thought it very strange that, as far as pizza went, I thought most people preferred thick crust (Chicago-style, I think they called it) with multiple toppings. "Most people around here think that thick crust stuff is horrible and would never order it," they said.

—L.K.

Case 26

The heat of the summer sun in the city is enough to bring most people to the edge. Well, on this particular day we decided to bring all of our kids to the park.

They were not the most well-behaved. But honestly, when you see kids getting beat down, where you feel like you have to board up your windows, your brother was shot in the head last year, and your mom brings you with her to neighborhood parties where you, a 9-year-old, watch everyone get lit...This group of 40 five-to 12-year-olds had behaved well enough to deserve the two-block walk over blazing concrete to our neighborhood park.

Our park was basically half a city block square with an asphalt football field, concrete basketball courts, handball courts, and one fountain that came on whenever the "parkie" felt like making the effort. (This day we were not so lucky.)

I don't particularly remember what Elijah had done or said, but I do remember his response to my asking him to stop. He started kicking and swinging and cursing in a really scary rage, especially for a nine-year-old. All I could do was wrap him up in my arms. He was furious and I was his straitjacket. And while receiving the verbal assault I haven't heard even from an adult, I held tight. I responded to each cut with "I love you."

After 10 minutes of his words of hatred and my words of love, I could feel his body slowly relax. I was all of a sudden holding a baby. I released him. He stood up, looked me in the eyes, and with a smile of total sincerity, said, "You wanna play ball?"

—Jay R.

Reflections on Cases 23-26

1) Which of these cases are you most drawn to? Why?

2) Robbins indicates that (youth) cultural awareness is very important to our understanding needs, being relevant without being relativistic, and as a means to help us move in and out of the culture we're trying to engage. Go back through each of the cases. In what respects did each of the authors attempt to do these three things? How successful were they?

3) When you were a teenager, did any Christian youth workers (church or parachurch, volunteer or paid) attempt to enter your world? What point of contact was there? How did you feel about their attempt to bridge the cultural gap? Were they successful? Why or why not?

FOR FURTHER DISCUSSION:

The Issue of Youth Subcultures

4) With some of your classmates, first think of and then portray in skit form at least five of the youth subcultures you are aware of. (If you want some help getting ideas, rent the classic '80s movie called *Three O' Clock High*. The subcultures portrayed there persist in most U.S. high schools to this day.)

5) What are some ways a youth worker who wants to reach young people in the subcultures you listed in question 4 can learn about these cultures and stay current with these cultures?

6) Prepare an annotated Internet bibliography of at least three secular and three Christian Web sites that will help the youth worker stay in touch with youth culture. (A google.com search will get you started.)

7) If you are 18 or 19 years old, being in touch with youth culture will seem easy. How, do you think, will you stay in touch with youth culture at age 29, 39, and 49? Do you think you will even care to stay in touch with youth culture when you're 49? Why or why not?

8) Robbins lists seven societal trends that are impacting and influencing youth culture today. From your own background and experience, which three would you say are the most important, and why?

For a Major Project or Paper

1) The study of youth subcultures is hugely important in youth ministry education in the United Kingdom. Some educators would go so far as to claim one cannot do youth ministry without significant academic training (if not a graduate degree) in cultural anthropology or culture studies. For example, see the master's program offered at King's College London (which is part of the University of London) at http://www. kcl.ac.uk.

   Compare and contrast youth culture websites from the United States and Britain. What valuable insights are there to be gained in this process?

2) See if you can obtain the missions training materials of a major faith mission or denominational missions arm. What changes would you need to make, if any, to the material to make it applicable to the reaching youth subcultures? Prepare, in outline form, materials you could use to teach this material to other youth workers.

3) Research a youth subculture that you would consider an "unreached people group." For example, obtain and read Marilyn Manson's *Long Dark Road Out of Hell* and at least gain a feel for the "listmania" books that come up when you search for Manson's book on amazon.com. Also explore "goth" Web sites and music. Given this research, what are ways a youth worker can enter the goth-Manson youth world and gain a hearing?

CHAPTER 9

READING THE WATER:
SCOUTING THE RIVER

WARM UP

This chapter will get you thinking about our culture in general and youth culture in particular. In England, many college students regularly watch *The Simpsons* and see it as an accurate portrayal of American culture. You may agree or disagree as to the cultural significance of the *The Simpsons*. What would you say are television programs or movies that depict important aspects of our society?

CASE STUDIES

Case 27

See case 7, (page 23) for one youth worker's attempt to do evangelism in a postmodern way.

Case 28

There were 30 kids, middle schoolers, there that night. I had decided that refreshments would be at the end of the night instead of right before the Bible study. (If given food just before Bible study time some of the kids would occupy their time by tearing their plastic cups into elaborate shapes and showing them to each other when the youth pastor was not looking in their direction.) I had them all gather on the carpeted floor facing the front rather than in a big "U" shape sitting on couches. Then I announced that Mark would be doing part of the teaching that night. The room grew silent and some jaws dropped.

Mark was an eighth-grade guy, a little on the rebellious side, and was frequently one of those we had to "sit on" to stop causing trouble in the group. Anyway, his part of the lesson was to tell the group a little about the town of Colossae, since it was from Paul's letter there that we were getting our verse for the night. When I approached him a few days earlier about helping to teach he was very surprised, and, I think, pleased. I told him there was plenty on the Internet about Colossae so he'd have no trouble getting information. Our verse had to do with right and wrong choices, so his report told about some of the choices available, such as going to a certain Roman temple to "worship" really meant you were going there to have sex with the girl-priests.

Had I been the one to tell the group about Colossae they probably would have listened, but under protest. With Mark up front they listened as they would to a rock star or movie celeb. It was interesting, because in the weeks that followed I noticed Mark was much more quick to settle down when we were finished with games and it was time for Bible study.

—L.K.

Reflections on Cases 27 and 28

1) If you are uncomfortable with the approach the author took in Case 27, what is it specifically that you are uncomfortable about?

2) Have you shared Christ in what you consider to be a postmodern way? What happened?

3) The author of case 28 was attempting to bridge the gap with these early adolescents by having a peer do some of the teaching, and it worked well. How would you have responded if you were part of that group and thought Mark was kind of a rebel?

4) What impacts of relativism or postmodernism have you observed in youth today?

FOR FURTHER DISCUSSION:

Secularism, Pluralism, and Postmodernism

5) Interview three or four youths. What do the words "popular culture" mean to them? How do they and their friends stay in touch with what is "cool"?

6) Do the exercise embedded in the Robbins text, Table 9-1.

7) Opposite that table Robbins says that some young Christians follow this philosophy: "If I feel okay it must be fine with Jesus." What examples have you seen? Upon reflection, does this statement reflect your own perspective?

8) Robbins lists some good features of postmodernism in the subsection "Introduction to Postmodernism." Which one or two do you most agree with and why?

9) Obtain two recent issues of *Teen People* and read them cover to cover. Find examples of popular culture, secularism, pluralism, and postmodernism.

10) Do the project "Mapping Out the Local Terrain."

For a Major Project or Paper

1) Robbins describes The Universal Quests in Table 9-2.

   a) Write a case study of your own adolescence, describing in detail at least one example from your own life illustrating your own quests for intimacy, identity, initiative, and immanence. Read the case studies of other class members. What similarities and differences do you see?

   (In items b,c,d, and e you may have to do some translating to help your interviewees understand what it is you mean by each of the four quests.)

   b) If possible, interview your grandparents, asking them to recall their own experiences of the four quests. Write them up as case studies.

   c) If possible, interview your parents about the quests. Write them up as case studies.

   d) Interview at least one 15-or 16-year-old. Ask the young person to talk about his or her own progress on the four quests. Write these up as case studies.

   e) Find one person, young or old, who is of a racial or ethnic background radically different from yours. Find out about this person's quests. Write these as case studies.

   Now, read over all your case studies, and those of other class members if possible. What themes do you see? What conclusions can you draw? What implications are there from your research for your own ministry to and with young people?

2) Obtain on DVD any complete season of *The X Files* you choose. Watch, perhaps with friends, at least five episodes. What examples do you find of secularism, pluralism, or postmodernism? Pick two of the main characters. Are they on any "quests"? Describe.

3) Compare and contrast the three books described in footnote 31: *The Empty Church* by Thomas Reeves (1996); *The Death of Character* by James Davison Hunter (2000); and *The Devaluing of America* by William J. Bennett (1992). From your study, prepare a 30-to 60-minute seminar, appropriate to be given to youth workers or parents. Feel free to illustrate your presentation with various examples of popular culture in various media.

CHAPTER 10

INTRODUCING THE CHURCH: HOLY GROUND OR UNHOLY GRIND

WARM UP

What is your earliest memory of being in church? What was your parents' attitude about church, and how was this conveyed to you as a child or young person?

Robbins' chapter is a great introduction to thinking about the church and its current state in our culture today. Now, let's think about doing youth ministry in the church context.

CASE STUDIES

Case 29

Dear Pastor Kageler,

With regards to your so-called youth rally next month, I am writing to inform you again that I feel what you have planned is a godless abomination. I am writing our national office and our Christian college presidents, as well as the other pastors in our district to ask them to join me in fasting and prayer, and to call upon God to stop this evil. You will be held accountable by almighty God for the deception and worldliness you are fostering among our precious young people.

I intend to do everything in my power to stop this event...

With the unanimous support of our elders, the youth rally went ahead as planned. Five hundred high school kids showed up, representing about 15 different churches. It was a multi-church Christian lip-sync competition and worship time. The entire night was student-led. The emcees were two seniors from our youth group; the guy wore a tuxedo and the girl a formal dress. Before each group lip-sync'd song, a performer told why they chose that song. There were some powerful testimonies that night. I found out later from other youth pastors who were present that two kids were dramatically saved that night, even though the night was definitely not an "outreach." During the worship time at the end, it seemed like heaven came down.

And in the back, through the little window of the sound room, I could see the lens of a video camera. I knew that Mr. Prescott, author of the hate mail given above, was behind that camera, making sure he gathered proper evidence for the hearing (trial? beheading?) he envisioned. Yes, we were allowing "music with a beat" to infect our young people. As far as he and some others in the church were concerned, this was no different from taking our youth on a trip to hell and leaving them there.

—L.K.

Case 30

I couldn't believe what I was hearing! I had been at this church six months serving as their part-time youth pastor while going to college to get a degree in youth ministry. I had done all the right things, or so I had thought. My ministry was "purpose driven." It was relational. That was the most fun for me, because I love just chillin' with the group. When I came, there were about 20 regular attenders, both junior and senior high combined.

So I'd spent the first six months doing what my youth ministry profs had said: build relationships with kids, get to know the parents, be a good communicator, show them you're competent and not a stupid fool, and love Jesus in the process. My profs said more than this, of course, but this is what I had time to do in my 12 or so hours per week. In addition to Sunday school, we had a weekly meeting on Sunday nights and a monthly fun thing. I did some small group discipleship training with those who really wanted to go deeper, too.

Now it was time to do some outreach. I wanted to help them reach their friends. First we talked about being comfortable just talking about spiritual things with our friends. Then we planned an outreach event. This event was not for high-powered evangelism, but at least it would be an invite-a-friend night where there would be ample fun and a chance for a couple of the kids to tell the group what a difference Jesus has made in their lives. One of the two testimony givers was a 14-going-on-21-year-old girl who could easily be on the front cover of Seventeen. She loved Jesus with all her heart and was nervous but excited to speak. I knew every guy in the room would listen to her, that's for sure.

But the event never happened.

Mr. Johnson, chairman of the board, pulled me aside a week before the event.

"Jim, you've planned and publicized this outreach event, right?"

I was expecting a "Nice job" or "We'll be praying for you!" Instead he said, "Cancel it."

I was speechless.

"Our youth ministry is for our kids, not their friends. We don't want outside influences in the group. The purpose of the group is to maintain and conserve our church family young people. This is our main focus here. Cancel this outreach event, and don't plan another one. Do I make myself clear?"

I was still speechless, and very sad.

—Mike

Reflections on Cases 29 and 30

1) What surprises you, and what doesn't, about these cases?

2) It looks like some of the people in the cases had different views of little words like "holy," "catholic," and "apostolic" as these words are discussed in Robbins' text. Elaborate.

3) What would be some things the authors both enjoy and dislike about church-based youth ministry?

4) If you had to write a case about an either positive or negative "youth ministry in the church" experience, what would it include?

FOR FURTHER DISCUSSION:

Reflecting On the Church and Youth Ministry

5) Robbins lists seven things about the church today (in the subsection "Examining the Body"), from hypocrisy through consumer-centeredness. Go through the list in a small group. How might youth in the church experience these, or how might youth ministry foster these negatives? Can you think of youth ministries that are the exact opposite of one or more of these items?

6) In Table 10-1, we see church as a spiritual day care, a fitness center, a cathedral, and a *M*A*S*H* unit. With others in the class, prepare a 5-10-minute segment from a typical youth group meeting that would reflect each of these four very different emphases.

7) If you were in a youth ministry as a teenager, which of the four styles comes closest to your experience?

8) Do you know any families with teenagers who have ever left your church, or another church, to come to yours? Why did they leave? If you were part of a youth ministry and church where new families with teenagers came, what brought them to your ministry?

For a Major Project or Paper

1) Do a thorough analysis of problems related to youth ministry in the local church. Start with an advanced google.com search using the phrase "problems in youth ministry." Then interview at least five youth pastors. Lastly, review the last two years worth of *Youthworker Journal* (Youth Specialties) or *Group* magazine for additional material. In all of this, what common themes do you find? Are the problems mainly stemming from poorly trained youth workers, or a dysfunctional church or senior pastor, or something else?

2) The footnotes in this chapter cite numerous excellent books about the state of the church. First, obtain and read at least two of them. Second, compare and contrast the content of these books. Third, suggest possible implications and applications for church-based youth ministry.

Unit 3:

Charting a Course For the Journey

CHAPTER 11

ADOLESCENT SPIRITUALITY:
THE ODYSSEY OF GROWING FAITH

WARM UP

When did you become a Christian? What were some things that influenced your own faith development, both positively and negatively, through middle and senior high school?

CASE STUDIES

Case 31

April was only 12 when her grandparents dropped her off at youth group one night for the first time. I was up in the youth room and didn't get to meet them. April followed some kids up the stairs. I looked up and there she was, standing at the youth room door. She apparently didn't know a soul, so I went over and greeted her. Over the next weeks she began to warm up to the group, and she was starting to fit in.

Over time I heard her sad story, told to me both by her and by her grandparents. April's parents didn't want her. She was fine as a cute little child, but her parents had no time or energy to deal with her emerging adolescence. Her parents lived in Los Angeles. Her mother, according to April, did something in Hollywood. Her father spent most of his time doing the Los Angeles–New York City commute.

Her parents finally decided to ship her North to Seattle to live with grandparents. April hated her mother, with whom she always fought. She liked and admired her father, however. He had taken her to New York a couple of times when she was younger. He also sent her lots of money. At age 12 she had more disposable income than many adults. She came to everything the youth group had on the calendar and eventually received Christ into her life at a Christian concert we went to.

I'm not usually an emotional person, but one night after youth group I noticed she was standing by herself and had tears running down her face. "What's wrong?"

"My birthday was two days ago. My parents forgot..."

I didn't sleep very well that night; my heart really breaking for a kid who was really turning out to be a wonderful person.

Some of the April's edges were beginning to smooth out, and the fruit of the Spirit began to show through. Karen, a female middle school volunteer, was meeting with April regularly to disciple her. April attended Sunday school eagerly and just seemed to want to soak it all in. She seemed to care a lot for her peers, without regard for "coolness." She brought good energy to the group as well.

One night I was teaching, and we were doing a series on spiritual gifts. Now the idea of spiritual gifts might be a stretch for middle schoolers generally, but I tried very hard to make illustrations and analogies to help it make sense. I was trying to draw an analogy to a house, our group, and spiritual gifts.

"Yes!" It was April, with a beaming smile. "I'm electricity in the house!"

—L.K.

Case 32

Ten of us from our ministry team were in another city for a week to learn and practice evangelism. On the first night, I had a revealing chat with 14-year-old Joshua. He had recently come back from a Christian camp and was motivated to read and study his Bible, especially those passages pertaining to the Second Coming of Christ. I asked Joshua a question I often ask my youth group members: "What do you want to do for a living after you finish school?" His reply was "to become a missionary." When I asked him why he wanted to go into ministry, he said the reason was that he didn't want to see people end up in hell.

During the rest of the week, he was true to his word. He was attentive at the seminars where we learned about evangelism and was joyous at the worship celebrations. When we went to the malls, Joshua and others, for the first time in their lives, boldly approached strangers and explained the gospel to them. And for the first time in their lives, several people prayed with them to receive Christ as their Lord and Savior!

But talking to strangers was the easy part. The hard part came later on that week when Joshua and the rest of us wrote our friends and relatives who were unbelievers to tell them we wanted to talk to them when we got back home about our relationship with God.

As the week went on, I told Joshua that I had seen him grow in Christ. His reply was that his growth began in June when he got baptized and continued in early July at the Christian camp to which his parents had sent him.

At the end of the week, the 10 of us did an exercise where we gave affirmations to one another. The Holy Spirit moved us unexpectedly that night as we allowed ourselves to become vulnerable. I wanted to pay Joshua the highest compliment I could, so I told him that it was because of him and others like him that I chose youth ministry as my vocation. In tears, Joshua said that he was an only child who sometimes feels lonely and who saw us as his second family.

When we got back home, Joshua followed up on the friends he had written. He brought a couple of them to our youth group meetings and events. But one of them, a Muslim, unfortunately told Joshua that he would not switch religions no matter what. Despite the apparent setback, Joshua continues to be friends with the young man, hoping to lead him to Christ.

Today, Joshua is a member of our drama ministry and our music ministry, even though he didn't think he could sing well. He's also active in another church during the times we don't have anything scheduled. His parents continue to be active members of our church and continue to make the sacrifices necessary to have their child participate in our activities and events. And today, I'm still a minister to youth (in the same downtown church!) after 10 years because of the Joshuas God gives me the privilege to impact and who, just as importantly, impact me.

—Bob

Case 33

What really changes kids spiritually? I've wondered and worked at that a lot over the years. I've spent hours with other youth pastors sharing ideas. The thing I enjoy most about being a youth pastor (even more than getting paid to ski or backpack!) is seeing leadership team kids get excited about ministry and feel like they're unleashed to serve him with enthusiastic joy.

At our twice-monthly leadership team meetings a lot of things are done, but the meeting always begins and ends the same way.

We begin with all 11 of us sitting in a circle. We take the first 30-45 minutes of our meeting doing several rounds of sharing. The first round is "Something good and something not so good in your life in the last two weeks." Second round is "Tell about your devotional life in the last week or so." Third round is: "Who have you spoken with in the last two weeks in youth group that you don't normally speak to?" Then we pray for each other about the things that have come up. If someone is really hurting we gather around and lay on hands in prayer. It has been great to teach kids what that symbolizes.

After training, planning, and reporting how each of our "five most wanted" friends are doing, we close with prayer, not for each other, but for the student ministry itself. We get the chairs in a circle, and we arrange them so we can kneel at them facing the center of the circle. Now our prayers are only for the ministry, and for God to show up in powerful ways. It has been so awesome to hear these students pray for what has become their ministry. I find this "knee-circle" prayer really, over time, changes their hearts toward the group. They grow spiritually to the point where, when they come to group, they come as givers, not takers. For another take on this turn to Case Study 13.

—L.K.

Reflections on Cases 31, 32, and 33

1) What ways do you see the authors of these cases trying to foster the spiritual growth of youth?

2) Which aspects of faith development theory fits with these cases? Describe.

3) If you were in a youth ministry as a youth yourself, was there a student leadership team of any sort? If so, how did your youth leader try to foster the team's spiritual growth? On the "Four Levels of Sanctification" chart (page 395) where did you begin and where did you end? How about the kids mentioned in these cases? Where would you place them on this same chart?

FOR FURTHER DISCUSSION:

Thinking About Spiritual Growth

4) Robbins lists seven axioms under the heading "True Spirituality." React to each.

5) In Axiom number four are listed some indicators of spiritual growth and change in youths, like stopping cursing or writing a note of apology. Did any of these specifics, or something like them, happen in your life in junior/senior high? What triggered this spiritual growth in you?

6) In what respect do you agree or disagree with the statement, "True spirituality requires an unchanging commitment to Jesus but what 'commitment to Jesus' looks like will be a matter of consistent change."

7) You probably were interested in "The Faithful Change" research project among Christian college students referred to in footnote 52. To what extent has each of the five made a difference, for better or worse, in your own spiritual development?

For a Major Paper or Project

1) Watch one of the movies from *The Lord of the Rings* trilogy and trace "faith development" as a subtext of the movie. What theories of faith development do you see manifested in the film? Elaborate.

2) Choose one of the five items from the "Faithful Change" research project (in the subsection "Faith Development and Developing Teenage Disciples," page 410). Express your understanding of that item in some form of visual media: clay, paint, collage, or even dance.

3) Connect Westerhoff's theories (Figure 11-2) to the concept of postmodernism. Explain and illustrate the connections you have found.

4) Prepare an annotated Internet bibliography with at least ten entries of websites designed to help youth grow spiritually.

5) Do a professional curriculum review of two youth-oriented spiritual development resources (Sunday school curriculum, discipleship resources, and so on). Include the following comparisons: a) age appropriateness, b) the role and place of scripture, c) clear lesson aim and objectives, d) ease of use for teachers, e) creativity and variety of teaching methods, f) general strengths/weaknesses.

CHAPTER 12

YOUTH MINISTRY ORIENTEERING:
DEVELOPING A PHILOSOPHY OF YOUTH MINISTRY

WARM UP

What are some examples of pursuits in which things are truly messed up if you don't have a clear purpose? For example, take the hoops away and think about playing basketball.

CASE STUDIES

Case 34

I had only been at the church for two months before realizing I had no clue what I was doing! I was frantically trying to come up with wild and crazy games that would entertain the multitudes. My lessons needed to be first-rate, a mixture between classic Billy Graham evangelism and a Sunday morning sermon. I knew that there would be a range of students attending our weekly youth group nights—some Christians with a desire to grow in their faith and some just wanting to hear the youth pastor say the word "sex."

The question that drove me wild and made my hands shake—or maybe it was all the caffeine—was how to reach so many different types of students at different spiritual levels in just one meeting.

The answer I discovered, or, should I say, was told to me by a wise veteran youth worker, was this: "You cannot, so…quit!" What he meant was quit trying to meet every need every night. I needed a purpose, a vision for my youth ministry and for my programs. So instead of just showing up each week and hoping that each student would benefit from my all-in-one weekly special (the Wal-Mart of church), I decided to stop what I was doing and think about why I was doing it.

My purpose behind becoming a youth pastor was simply to help students to know Jesus and make him known. There were two aspects: outreach and discipleship. But in order to do both the best I could, I needed specific purposes behind each event and each night. Otherwise, as I learned from experience, my weeks got frustrating, and discouragement overtook my life and ministry.

So, I came up with three goals and purposes and then modeled everything we did after those. 1) See nonbelievers come to Jesus as Lord and Savior. 2) Develop fully devoted followers of Christ. 3) Proclaim the good news of Christ to Westchester, New York, and beyond.

I set the vision and thought about what steps needed to happen in order to accomplish this. Since I still had no clue about how to write a purpose statement, let alone how to implement one, I decided to do what every youth pastor must do...cheat. Well, not really. I went looking for the best source on ministry, something called *How to Write a Purpose Statement in a Week and Have a Really Good Looking Youth Ministry*.

Okay, that book does not exist...yet. Here's what I did do.

I looked at Christ's own ministry and used the Great Commandment and Great Commission as the base for my purpose statement (hey, what better source, I thought!).

Within these two challenges I found a call to devotion, discipleship, fellowship, ministry, and evangelism. So I figured that our youth ministry should be involved in each of those. Here's what I came up with that fit the needs of our church and our youth:

"The youth ministry at BCC exists to help students connect with other believers, grow in their relationship with God, worship the Lord through their lives, serve others through ministry and missions, and reach the community and world for Christ."

So, my leaders, our students, and I all know what each program, activity, and event is meant to accomplish. Sunday mornings are our time for growth through teaching God's Word. Sunday night small groups provide students an opportunity to continue on the path of discipleship through worship, fellowship, and accountability. We also have service projects and missions trips to get our students involved in ministry. Then our weekly youth group nights are for outreach, and so the lessons and atmosphere are geared with that one purpose in mind.

People now can see that all our programs meet specific needs and say "Wow, look at their successful programs." But I know that these programs are only as good as the purposes behind them.

—Dan

Case 35

Two years into my ministry things really seemed to be taking off. Three years into it I was ready to quit.

When I first arrived at my new church, I brought with me creativity, enthusiasm, and excitement. The change was well-received. Under the old youth pastor, the youth ministry had become a place even senior citizens would have found dull. So here I was, the self-proclaimed "savior" of the youth group…or so I thought. I must admit the initial out-with-the-old, in-with-the-new transition time was rather difficult. After all, I had to excommunicate all the "former" youth leaders and start my reign as the Hussein of Youth Group, ruling with an iron fist. Well, not exactly.

I got to know the students, leaders, and parents, and I discovered the youth culture of this new city. Coming fresh out of college with a degree claiming that I knew how to do youth ministry, I got off to a great start. High Octane is what I called it. It probably helped that there was a coffee shop on every block and a snack shop in our church.

I could relate to the students, be "cool" in front of their friends, and come up with plenty of unique games and activities. Even the lessons were fine-tuned, almost like an art form. We had new students coming each week and our group nearly tripled by the end of the first year. The second year started off with a bang…literally. I broke a window in our church chasing after some student with a water gun.

So the year went well, but towards the end I started to feel the hype and excitement disappearing. I was scratching my head for new lessons. The ones I stole from my youth ministry classes were all used up. Some unchurched students were coming on Sunday mornings and feeling like they had just walked into a cult meeting, while my core students were getting frustrated at the lack of depth in our ministry.

Needless to say, by the end of my third year our group was still around the same size, minus a few frustrated and confused students, but there was no growth. I realized that the students I had inherited had only grown closer to each other and not to the Lord. I had failed at my most important task.

Confused, I started to ask around to get a feel for what had happened. The general response of my students and leaders was that they never really knew what was going on or where we were heading as a youth group. There was no vision, no plan, no purpose for them to grab hold of and make their own. They were ready for growth, but I was not prepared.

From that experience I learned the value of having a purpose behind everything, from my teachings to the reasons for our weekly youth group meetings. My lessons, youth group nights, and Sunday mornings were not focused because there were no specific goals or purposes guiding them. They were not achieving anything significant because I never thought about what I wanted them to achieve in the first place. I got away with that for a while, but like always, it caught up with me. I had sacrificed long-term planning for short-term success but finally learned a valuable lesson: "Where there is no vision or purpose, youth ministries perish." I guess I should have paid more attention in my Old Testament Wisdom Literature class.

—Dan

Case 36

Eric, our middle school youth pastor, stared blankly ahead, looking at no one. His face was flushed and his lips were tight. He said it again, his voice cracking in a weird combination of sadness and anger.

"We should have shared the gospel!"

The rest of us on the pastoral staff looked at Jim, our senior pastor. We liked to call Jim Augustus. Kind of an affectionate nickname. We called the senior pastor before him Big Toad (I was Adolescent Toad, Pete was Family Toad, Jill was Children's Toad, and so on). But this was not the time for humorous nicknames.

Jim looked squarely at Eric.

"Eric, you've been here six months. You've been in on the planning of last Sunday from day one. You haven't voiced a syllable of opposition or question. Your anger now is a little confusing."

Jim had been on the scene for 18 months and was trying to help the church get beyond being a kind of club for Christians toward being more outreach-focused and "seeker sensitive." We started a contemporary worship service, which, by the way, came only after considerable bloodletting (metaphorically speaking, of course) and several families had left the church because of it. But with those families gone, the church leadership seemed much freer and more open to change and the leading of a visionary senior pastor.

What we had just done, and what Eric was so upset about, was to have a "welcome Sunday" in which 200 visitors showed up to church. The (contemporary) service was awesome (in my humble opinion) and Pastor Jim's sermon was essentially an invitation to think about one's spiritual life and to consider the possibility that in this church there might be some answers to life's questions. It was deliberately "soft sell" and the congregation had been well-prepared for this. Eric was really fried because we did not do a gospel presentation and give an invitation or altar call.

How did we get 200 new people to show up on one Sunday? We believed what marketing people say: if you phone 20,000 people, 2,000 will want more information and 200 will "buy." So, with much prayer of course, that's what we did. We had 30 phone lines temporarily installed in a huge room at the church and over a two-week period from 6 p.m. to 9:30 p.m. each night church members sat at the phones calling the 20,000 listings within a five-mile radius of our church. I was involved in this phoning too and found the experience quite energizing. Sure enough, about 2,000 wanted to receive more information via a special mailing we had prepared, and about 200 new people actually showed up at our service.

Jim's message that Sunday was essentially an invitation for these new people to come back and "check it out." We had small groups and various other ministries that were customized to be newcomer-friendly.

Eric continued. "It was such a waste to have those people here and not give them the gospel. Many of them we'll never see again. It was just wrong. It was a missed opportunity. All our efforts were a waste of time."

—L.K.

Case 37

My wife and I were excited to start a new ministry together. We were leaving a thriving middle school ministry of over 120 kids to move to a fledgling ministry and take it to the next level. We were excited to work with a church that was committed to outreach, creativity, and doing whatever it took to connect with the next generation. During the interview process we clearly and thoroughly laid out our philosophy of ministry. We explained how we followed Christ's principles of ministry in trying to reach people at their different levels of spiritual interest and maturity. The church seemed excited about our three-to five-year plan for building a healthy youth ministry. We were anxious to get going.

However, the problems started to creep in slowly and then grew bigger and bigger. Our philosophy was to focus on reaching the reached before reaching the unreached. In other words we desired to develop those students who claimed to be Christ followers before intentionally beginning to reach out to those who don't know Christ. We wanted to equip students to reach students. We had observed in the past that an excited, growing, passionate, Christ-following teen was much more effective at evangelism and discipleship than any program ever could be.

We found that this was going to be difficult to accomplish for a couple of reasons. The first was that we discovered that in the five years previous to our arrival this church had had four different youth pastors (something that was unclear in the interview process). This caused the kids to become distant, hurt, broken, apathetic, and distrusting of us because they were certain we weren't going to be around very long. We tried really hard to love and lead these kids in their brokenness to bring them and the ministry to a place of healing.

The second reason was more significant. The senior pastor shared our overall desire for evangelism and for growth. However, it became apparent that our approaches and motivations were radically different. It was communicated regularly to us that it was his desire to build a large-scale youth group. We were pressured to have big outreach events, concerts, and the like to attract the masses. We had done big outreaches in our previous ministry, but it was always an extension of a healthy group that was ready for growth and would be a welcome home for those who needed Christ. I felt that emotionally and spiritually our students weren't ready for that kind of pressure. We also did not have enough trained adult leaders available to help shepherd the kids we already had even without adding more students to the group.

We quickly became aware that growth in numbers was the bottom line, not just in the youth ministry but also throughout the whole church. Bible teaching and a biblical presentation of the gospel was compromised in order to bring in more and more people. My personal bottom line was to lead a hurting, dysfunctional group to become a spiritually healthy group, that would be passionate about leading their friends to Christ.

We spent awhile trying to work through some of these differences with the pastor in an attempt to reach an understanding, but we soon realized it was his way or the highway. We discovered that we weren't going to be able to do what we felt God was leading us to do if we remained in this situation. After seeking the Lord, we felt that for the sake of unity of the church, and for our own spiritual health, we needed to leave. We have been gone for five years now and the church has had another four youth pastors come and go during that time. My heart breaks for those kids who have been hurt by a good vision gone bad.

—Kevin

Reflections on Cases 34-37

1) Robbins' chapter speaks of the importance of a clear philosophy of ministry, mission, values, et cetera. What were the consequences in case 35 of these being missing?

2) In cases 36 and 37 what were the frustrations of there being differing views of mission/purpose?

3) From what you have read in case 36, list what you can infer about any two of the following: philosophy of ministry, mission, core values, vision, or strategy.

FOR FURTHER DISCUSSION:

Thinking About "Setting Coordinates"

4) If you've ever been part of a youth ministry that was a "Lost Adventure" (see story at beginning of chapter) tell about it.

5) Survey several youth ministry mission-vision statements. Google.com "youth ministry mission statement" will give you quite a selection. Another source is youthpastor.com. Click on Resource Directory and then Youth Group Names. Over 4,000 youth group names are listed, most of which also have a website. It won't take you long to find some with mission-vision-values statements. How do the ministries you've chosen reflect well or poorly some of the concepts in this chapter?

6) If you are in a youth ministry right now, and it has a mission, vision, or values statement, compare and critique it from examples and insights in the chapter.

7) If you are in a youth ministry right now and it does not have a mission, vision, or values statement, in what ways (if any) do you think things would improve if it did?

8) As you anticipate youth ministry in your future, what will be some of your own core values? In what way might this reflect your own personality and gifting?

For a Major Project or Paper

1) Select 5-10 youth ministry mission, vision, or values statements and analyze them in terms of DeJong (Table 12-1).

2) Find five television or movie clips that illustrate lack of vision, purpose, core values, or strategy. Explain the connection to your classmates. Make a copy for your professor to keep.

CHAPTER 13

CHARTING A PLAN:
PHILOSOPHY OF PROGRAMMING

WARM UP

Have you ever been part of a youth program that went horribly wrong? What went wrong?

CASE STUDIES

Case 38

Even though this happened 10 years ago, it is still painful just to think about. My heart and vision were right, but, yikes, it didn't work out anything like I thought it would.

I interviewed with and accepted the call of one church to be their youth pastor in November, with a projected start date of mid-February. My mind began working overtime as to ways to have a strong first year. I had the mission-vision-core values and strategy thing down pretty well, and that actually led me to start planning a major outreach event there for my first October. I figured by then we'd have a core of kids who were ready to invite friends to something really cool and work hard to pull the whole thing off.

So, in December I made the arrangements for a very well-known Christian female (rock star) singer to come with her band and dance team for an October outreach concert. I was pleased to get that accomplished in such a short time, because I knew that people like her generally were booked two to three years in advance. Contract signed, I knew I could work on the rest of the details once I actually arrived on the scene at my new church.

In the next 10 months many things went wrong. The slick promo posters they promised didn't arrive until one week before the concert. I was shocked by the specificity and complexity of their light and sound requirements, and I worked to find a local provider at a reasonable cost. The band manager, two weeks before the concert, fired my provider and hired a different one. I learned from my own youth group and from the youth pastors in the area that Christian contemporary music was kind of a foreign idea in the area.

The day of concert was horrible. The sound and light people arrived to set up at 4 p.m. instead of 9 a.m. We quickly found out the middle school auditorium didn't have enough electrical power for their systems, so at 4:30 p.m. I was tracking down the school district head electrician. The good news was he agreed to run cable from the main something-or-other to the auditorium, but the bad news was that he charged $100 per hour. The singer and nine-member band flew in from Nashville and were taken to their hotel. Two of my youth group kids accompanied the vans that went to pick them and their stuff up. These two kids came to the auditorium while we were (frantically now) setting up and reported, "She's a witch. What a stuck-up snob!"

The night of the concert was worse yet. The band arrived on time but the sound and light people weren't ready. When I did a mental survey of the entourage I asked their road manager, "Where are the dancers your promo stuff bragged about?"

"Oh, that was last year's show. We don't have them anymore."

The sound check started at 8 p.m. when the concert was supposed to begin. So, we had 450-500 people standing outside for over an hour. Thank God it wasn't raining. I was thankful I had hired local police for security. Police presence did have a calming effect on impatient kids.

The concert finally started at 9 p.m. Financially, our break-even point was 750. I had hoped and prayed for 1,000. We had 500, max. I realized we would lose at least $6,000 that night.

"There goes my youth budget for the year, if not my life!" But I consoled myself in that it would all be worth it for the kingdom harvest we were about to experience.

The audience was enjoying the concert, but at about 45 minutes Ms. Star Singer began giving her "talk" and then her "invitation." I assumed this was the halfway point in the program. The only kids who "came forward" were my student leadership team kids, who we had agreed would come up to counsel with the others who came forward. Not one person made any response to the gospel presentation. The final song was sung and it was over and done at 10 p.m. One hour!

—L.K.

Case 39

After a few years of being a youth pastor I began to really think about this problem: A youth group meeting to which most kids in the ministry come—not for spiritual growth, but for fun. Is it possible to meet the needs of kids at different spiritual levels in the same meeting?

I got an idea and shared it with the student leadership team. They thought it was worth a try, so I got it approved by the CE committee and had a parent meeting to explain the philosophy of it.

Basically, I wanted to figure out how to "get rid of" the kids who were not interested in spiritual growth. I figured if I could just gather the ones who were wanting to grow, God would also show up, and stuff would start to happen. This life, I reasoned, would be attractive to the other youths, who then would also be motivated to attend a place where God was really obviously visible.

You're probably thinking, "Its simple, stupid. Just have one night for fun and outreach, and another night for spiritual growth, worship, and discipleship." It couldn't happen at this church, though, because the teens came from a 300-square-mile radius (26 different high schools) and one night a week was all I could reasonably pull off.

So, we tried a First Half-Second Half format.

First Half was "light." We got into our teams (the whole student ministry was divided into teams of 30 kids, each with three adult staff and three student leaders) for welcome, intro of newcomers, announcements related to team activities and so on. Then we did some kind of team competition, either involving whole teams or representatives. Next were funny announcements for the whole group, and then it was time for the Bible lesson. Whoever taught made it "light," fully aware that there were non-Christians or marginal Christians present. After that came halftime, during which refreshments were served and the music was up.

Then came Second Half. The kids had several choices: play volleyball or basketball in the gym, play ping pong or pool in another room, hang out in the parking lot, or be in the "serious" part of Second Half, which involved worship, prayer, small groups, and going deeper in the Bible study. We had a schedule for our volunteer staff to rotate through these various choices over the course of a typical month.

Our first night only the leadership team kids were in the serious part of Second Half, as expected. But we had a powerful time, and within three months 90 percent of those who came on Wednesday nights chose to be in the serious part of Second Half. Kids' lives were being changed; God was definitely doing things.

I tried this change at my next church (also home of my outreach concert disaster described in case 39) and the very same thing happened. There, the first time we did the First Half-Second Half thing, a senior girl came up to me afterwards in tears.

"I have been here almost every Wednesday night for nearly four years, and this is the very first time I have ever felt God here, too." Amen! Same ratios happened there too. We began with a 10 percent to 90 percent split, serious to non-serious. Three months later 90 percent of those who came were in the serious part of Second Half, while only 10 percent chose the other options.

—L.K.

Case 40

I enjoy thinking of ways to help kids minister and serve. So in one church I served, I thought, "Why not go Christmas caroling on Porno Row downtown?" I'm not kidding. It would bring some light into a very dark place, and it would also help our kids, especially the Christian school kids, get a feel for what it is like to be pressured or persecuted.

I explained my crazy idea to the pastoral staff, the student leadership team, and then the CE Committee and a meeting of parents. I'd already been at the church five years and had built a reputation of trust and reasonableness. People listened to my idea skeptically at first, but eventually everyone thought it might be a great idea. I knew full well that this was an event that 150 kids would not show up to. I would be happy with 20 or 30, plus lots of staff and parents. I notified the local police precinct of our plans, and had assurances the officers on the street and those patrolling in cars would be aware of our presence.

The night went great! The street was full on the Friday night we went. Patrons coming in and out of these places or just walking the sidewalks had all kinds of reactions. We got ignored, applauded, sworn at, leered at, blessed, and thanked. We went out for pizza afterwards and everyone felt the experience was a good one.

Our next year we were there on the streets again. Leading the singing for us was a 16-year-old girl, Marisa, who was an excellent leader in all respects. One X-rated place we sang for had the front door open. We could see a lady standing inside behind a counter who was obviously enjoying our singing. When we were finished, she came out and handed Marisa a Christmas stocking. Marisa was so pleased, gave the lady a hug, and turned around to face all of us. We assumed it was full of Christmas candy. Marisa opened the stocking as we all looked on, and it was filled with…flavored condoms, handcuffs, a whip, and a few things even I didn't recognize.

—L.K.

Case 41

Our mission statement is to minister to teens at their level of spiritual interest and maturity. Our strategy is to partner with students and staff to pursue programming that transcends the diversity of spiritual interest and maturity.

As I got off the phone after booking a Christian comedian, I was excited, because I knew we had a winner of a night planned for inviting friends to our program. I was convinced that I was about to give our teens the opportunity of their lives to influence their nonchurched friends.

Our attendance that night more than doubled for both middle school and senior high teens. I was excited to see many of our "fringe kids" show up, but I was disappointed that only a few of our teens actually invited non-church friends. Our guest did a great job of keeping us laughing at ourselves and even wove some dynamic spiritual truths into his endless humor. I left excited that we had had such a great night, but disappointed thinking many kids had missed out on an opportunity.

Sitting in my La-Z-Boy at home, unwinding after the event, I received a call from one of my key leader guys. He was almost out of breath as he asked, "How much did it cost to bring in the comedian guy? He was great, and I want to bring him back so I can invite my friends. I would even invest my own money." I quickly replied, "So you really didn't trust me, did you?" He said, "I trust you, but I didn't trust the comedian because of his funny name."

—Joe

Reflections on Cases 38-41

1) Robbins' chapter refers to a philosophy of programming that targets youth according to their level of commitment. What are the target youth populations for cases 38, 39, and 40?

2) In case 39, the author is trying to deal with the "no target/low aim" (Robbins page 506) principle.

What other solutions have you seen or can you think of that deal with this issue? What do you think of case 39 as a solution?

3) What mistakes did the author of case 38 make? Place yourself in the shoes of the youth pastor at the end of that horrible night. Assuming you wouldn't resign and start a career at Starbucks or Home Depot, how would you deal with the aftermath in the next several weeks?

4) In what way does case 41 exemplify an awareness of the principles spoken of in Robbins' chapter?

FOR FURTHER DISCUSSION:

Thinking About Our Personhood, Our Pursuit

5) React to Robbins' suggestions about The Ministry of Incarnation (page 472ff.). Which do you find the most helpful and why?

6) Robbins mentions that sometimes numerical growth is "limited by systems." Have you ever seen this happen? With what little you know about the student ministry described in case 39, in what respects can you see it is a system designed to accommodate numerical growth?

7) Missionaries love the Engel Scale (Figure 13-2); so do those who long to reach youth subcultures. Mentally take the roof off a middle or high school you know of, and in your mind's eye, picture where the different youth subcultures gather. Pick one or two of these subcultures. Where might they be on the Engel Scale? Where were you on the same scale at ages 12, 15, and 17?

8) Pick a student ministry you know well. Match up its program components to the target youth audience in terms of "pyramid of commitment" (Figure 13-5).

For a Major Project or Paper

1) Go back through all 41 cases in this Companion Guide. Just about every one can be matched, either by kid or by program component, to the "pyramid of commitment" model (Figure 13-5). Make those matches and explain the connection you see.

2) Go back to the Web site youthpastor.com, click on Resource Directories and then Youth Group Names. Check out at least 10 youth ministry Web sites that show their different program offerings. Match the program components to "levels of commitment" and explain your choice.

3) Personally visit several youth ministries and make brief videos of different program components. (Remember to get permission from the youth leader. Also, notice should be given to the youth group members' parents as well.) Then group the clips according to the programs' purpose according to the pyramid model (Figure 13-5).

CHAPTER 14

Assembling a Team

WARM UP

When you were in high school, were you ever in a band, play, or on a sports team? What are some things that made being a part of that "team" a positive or negative experience?

CASE STUDIES

Case 42

Read the letter Robbins received from a youth worker, under "Burden and Blessing" at the beginning of the chapter.

Case 43

I had been "on the ground" in my new church only a week when the chairman of the youth committee took me to lunch. He had been overseeing the youth staff in the months between the firing of the previous youth pastor and my arrival in April.

"This is the happiest day of my life." He smiled at me and pulled out a six-foot pile of file folders. One by one he handed them to me.

"This is Day Camp...did you know you're in charge?"

"This is the Grad Banquet."

"This is Summer Camp."

Now the pile of eight separate files sat in front of me. I felt a little overwhelmed, to say the least. Over the next three months all five couples of the youth committee resigned. They were "too busy" or "felt called" to another ministry in the church. I recruited one other couple during that time, but they soon resigned as well, saying, "We don't feel you communicate with us very well." Words to ponder.

I had an epiphany one evening. It was middle school night, and my arms were chock-full of supplies I was carrying from my office down to the gym. Jennifer, a mother who was on the volunteer team for junior high, looked at me sadly and said, "Don't you even trust us to carry the sports equipment?"

Later that first year I was taken to lunch by a board member, who worked as an executive "head hunter." I guess he did business around the world because he traveled a lot. He had a kid in the youth group, however, and actually showed up to help from time to time. His house was huge, too, and it included an indoor pool, so the youth group had events at his place occasionally. Eventually he paused. My heart was racing.

"You know, I've watched you now for a year as our youth pastor," he said. "You're really good with kids, but you're not good at all with adults who want to work with kids. I want to help you get to where you need to be when it comes to ministry skills for working through volunteers. If you don't upgrade your skills here, it's only a matter of time before you crash and burn."

—L.K.

Case 44

I usually paid pretty close attention to attendance. By now we had a couple of hundred kids in the middle school and senior high groups. A software guy in our church designed a special attendance-tracking software for us. Each month at our meetings my staff would receive a printed report of their own subgroup and the attendance of each kid in that group for Sunday school, youth group, and other events for that given month. (A volunteer spent a morning each week doing data entry.)

I looked over the whole list and was surprised to see that Julie was, all of a sudden it seemed, coming very regularly to her eleventh-grade Sunday school class. She had a very sporadic attendance pattern previously but was now coming every week. That made me smile.

That is, until Julie's parents approached me one Sunday after the second service.

"Have you heard the news?"

"What's up?" I replied.

"Julie ran off with her Sunday school teacher last week and got married to him. They'll be back in a few weeks. I wonder if she'll finish high school?"

—L.K.

Case 45

Everyone loved Ramone. He was outgoing, played the keyboard like an extension of himself, and was amazingly creative. Ramone was 22 and a faithful volunteer in our senior high ministry. As I said, everyone loved Ramone, but apparently some *really* loved him.

"Hi, this is Samantha."

I always liked it when Sam called. She was on the student leadership team and a great example of a godly girl.

"There's something you need to know. I've been going out with Ramone in the last few months. We've kissed, but nothing else. I just found out that he has been going out with Kristen and Lorina too, all three of us, at the same time. He has been kissing them too. The three of us just figured this out today. We've all agreed to break up with him, but I just thought you'd want to know."

—L.K.

Case 46

The volunteer staff and I got to know and enjoy each other so much that we had to be careful not to ignore the kids when we were at youth group events. At our monthly meetings we usually began with supper and then prayed for each other. After our planning and training were over, we finished by praying for the youths themselves and the ministry. Then it was dessert time, which was followed by hot tub time. Hot tubs were ubiquitous at two of the three churches I served, so it wasn't hard to meet at a home with one. Some of us could stay late, soaking into the night. Hot tubs are outside, of course, and we all especially enjoyed walking through snow to get to this warm, soothing goal.

On one of our senior high winter retreats one of the vehicles broke down, so we were a couple of hours behind schedule. Close to midnight we still were miles from our destination. As the bus was winding through the dark countryside almost all the kids fell asleep, so the staff migrated to the front of the bus. We laughed, told stories, did some singing, and got louder and sillier as the miles went by. When we finally exited the highway the street lights illuminated the kids we cared for so much, as well as all of us. The unity and joy we felt in ministry made it definitely a "Kumbaya" moment.

—L.K.

Reflections on Cases 42-46

1) Robbins refers to working with volunteer staff as a "burden and blessing" (page 519). Find examples of both in cases 42-46.

2) The author of case 42 managed to (somehow) stay sane through the crises. What would you infer would need to be true of someone's life as a youth pastor to continue to function despite an unfolding and ongoing stressful situation?

3) What insights from Robbins' chapter could have prevented, or at least made less likely, the sad scenarios of cases 44 and 45?

4) Cases 43 and 46 are from the same ministry, just at different points in time. (Some years had elapsed between 43 and 46.) What are some things the author has apparently learned over those years?

FOR FURTHER DISCUSSION:

People Are the Plan

5) You may be taking this course at age 19 or 20, and sometimes it may seem that it is hard enough to get one's own act together, let alone think about leading and inspiring other peers or older adults. Take an honest look again at the "attitude competencies" found on page 528. Where are you with regard to each of these? Rate yourself on a 1-5 scale, with "1" meaning you haven't even thought about this until now and "5" meaning, "Honestly, I'm so good at this I can teach it."

6) Robbins raises "concerns" that people have about being a volunteer in youth ministry: lack of knowledge, that the job will never end, and fear of teenagers (beginning on page 530). Evaluate his "remedies." If you've had the chance to experience or at least observe a youth pastor trying to manage these three concerns and supply some kind of remedy, share it.

7) Included in the chapter is a list of eight items Doug Fields suggests are "red flags" about potential volunteers. In association with some friends in your class, role play these for the benefit of other class members. Have them guess which "red flag" each person represents.

8) If you have served under someone in a ministry or even a part-time secular job, evaluate their people management skills in terms of call, court, coach, and cover (page 544). Be specific about the positive and negatives you observed.

9) Find a movie clip that portrays a good example of teamwork, or not.

For a Major Project or Paper

1) Go to amazon.com and search "volunteers." From the list of books (1,700-plus!) or from a listmania, if featured, choose 10 books on volunteers that are rated five stars by readers. From all the information you can click on for each of these books, compare and contrast them. Obtain one of them and prepare your notes for a 45-minute teaching seminar on the book's application to youth ministry staff recruitment.

2) Write a paper or prepare a 45-minute seminar that discusses the similarities of coaching a sports team to that of leading a staff of volunteers in youth ministry. Cite at least five books as resources as well as five Internet sites.

3) Go to questia.com and search "volunteers" or "managing volunteers." Choose your five favorite resources available from this source and write a thorough description of each, complete enough so your peers could decide to obtain this source or not if they were writing a paper on the subject.

APPENDIX 1

A Bowl of Beans for Your Birthright: Trading Away Theology

Amy Jacober, Ph.D.

Assistant Professor of Christian Education, Seattle Pacific University

A bowl of beans for your birthright. This seems like such a ridiculous trade with the benefit of hindsight. Esau was a hunter and worked in the fields. He was a busy, hard-working man. Jacob was a peaceful man, and was not as likely to be roaming the countryside. When both were doing what they did best, the arrangement worked.

I can only imagine what the day was like. Esau had been out, again. He came back home full of stories, exhausted, trying to keep too many things straight in his head and was going for the quick fix. Jacob had been home all day and had just what Esau needed. Jacob, however, did not freely offer. Esau, feeling overwhelmed and tired (to the point where he says he's gonna die!), goes for the quick fix, sells his birthright and settles down for a nice bowl of lentil stew (Genesis 25:27-34).

A bowl of beans for your birthright. Maybe this wouldn't tempt you, but would the latest games? The coolest music or DVD? Counseling techniques? A sure-fire curriculum? An evangelism program? Social activism? The list could go on and on and on... As youth ministers, we are not that far from Esau. We spend our time with kids, we run from staff meeting to basketball game to Sonic for hang-out time, and when it comes time to lead a group, to teach on Sunday, to plan a retreat, we are tired. And this is for those of us who are lucky enough to do this full-time. Add in that the majority are full-time somewhere else, as students or working, and our plates are full.

"Jacob, do you have another lesson I can prepare in 30 minutes or less, including a video clip to make me look like I know what's going on in the world today?" "Jacob, I have a student in crisis, do you have anything that will let me become her social worker?" "Jacob, do you have something I can study to learn the latest movies and music that can help me connect?" There are more than enough resources out there to offer a "yes" answer to these questions.

I am a product of, and have become a perpetuator of, a generation of Christians who are scripturally illiterate and theologically void. I deeply respect and love the man who was my youth minister and do not want to seem ungrateful for how God used him in my life. Most of my years as a student were spent being told and then reminded that God loved me and Jesus died for me, and to ponder what that means. Discipleship or any doctrine beyond salvation was rarely mentioned.

I am not saying this is the case for everyone, but I do not think I am as unique as I wish I were. I remember sitting in seminary and the professor making reference to Daniel and the lions' den. I also remember thinking to myself "Well, huh...I heard that story when I was a little girl at VBS...I haven't heard it in a long time, I wonder where it is?" Not exactly an obscure reference. I thank God daily for the table of contents and concordance in my Bible. If it were up to me these would be canonized as well. I have felt stupid more often than not at not knowing where to find something in the Bible, at not even knowing how to state my doctrinal position (truth be told, it took a long time before I could even explain what the word doctrine meant, let alone talk about specific ones).

We're not exactly encouraged to take theology seriously, though (thankfully) this is changing. Still, a church would rather hire a youth worker with a heart for kids, a little knowledge on how to budget and create a calendar or flyer and learn which curriculum to order to maintain the smooth ministry within that church, than to hire one who has a firm grasp of theology but no practical abilities. (You only have to go as far as web postings for youth ministry jobs to figure that one out.) We have been taught both formally and through expectations of the church that it is better to throw a good party with lots of adolescents than to have a deep conversation with one.

My academic background is in social work and theology. The more I did youth ministry, the more I thought I needed social work. I managed to end up with only a handful of "healthy" students, instead being led to drug-using, lying, Wicca-practicing, abused, gang-affiliated, poverty-stricken kids who came with the regular set of adolescent issues as well. I was frequently overwhelmed, out there working hard and looking for what could get a teenager (and me) to the next day. I was more than willing to ask any Jacob I could find for short-term fulfillment and forgot that long-term sustenance was the goal. Ironically what I learned in studying social work is that there are a lot of social workers out there. That led me to truly realize there are a lot of teachers, coaches, counselors, musicians, and a whole host of people who do what they do much better than I can. Most of them are not trying to be ministers, and yet as ministers, we do try to be them.

I am not saying that you can't be informed in any other area apart from theology. I'm saying simply that, at one point, I was giving up my birthright. I focused more on how to help a student and his family in the here and now than how to walk with them for permanent change, to perform the ministry that was my birthright. Social work was a point of God-given passion that took over my role as youth worker. Being the entertainer, the cultural guru, the game master, and the trip planner became more attractive than my role as a theologian-in-residence for a group of teenagers. And who could deny that the results of these as a focus were more immediate, and occasionally more gratifying? The common thought is that theology is too theoretical and has no relevance for meeting the needs of kids. Of course no one says this in an article, but look through the bookstores and catalogs, go to most (not all) training meetings. It's hard not to walk away with this thought. I talk with students and youth workers all the time who say they are really not into theology, they just want to love kids. When I ask what they mean, they say getting caught up in theology leads to division and denominations. While this sounds logical and right, it also leads to youth ministers meeting every need of kids save those of spirituality. It is not done with ill intentions. In fact, typically, it's not done intentionally at all.

David Livermore says, "The best choice for preparing youth ministers cannot be to decide between theory and practice. Theory and practice, or engagement and reflection, also known as praxis, are needed simultaneously." Youth ministers come with a variety of gifts and backgrounds. These are a blessing and should not be abandoned. But, ironically, we have in the process abandoned our birthright as a theological voice. Theology is not intended to be an irrelevant exercise in academic gymnastics. It is our faith, guided by the questions of our day, seeking understanding from God. For the youth minister, these are the questions which arise from looking more closely at the lives and culture of the adolescents whom we are called to serve. That is why, "when all is said and done, theology has to be at the core of how one prepares for youth ministry."

As youth workers we are trying to minister to adolescents to the best of our abilities, but there is a relatively slim body of literature and training that brings together theology and the other disciplines. One place to bridge the issue flows from the incarnation: God himself being fully divine and fully human. He never gave up the divine as he stepped out of heaven to enter this world. Accepting our birthright as ministers instead of looking to the birthright of others can be transforming! In my case, it was a natural result of my putting Christ at the center of my practical theology.

It is a lot of work, and it moves ministry far beyond the Wednesday night gathering and pizza party. But God set the pattern. As we open our eyes and allow scripture and doctrine to marinate our hearts, the words will come, teenagers will be blessed, and God will be honored.

For Reflection and Discussion

1) What is the main point of Dr. Jacober's article? Do you agree? Why or why not?

2) Choose one of the following decidedly theological notions:

   a) God is creative (He is creative after all!)

   b) People are messed up (sinful)

   c) God longs to communicate with people.

Imagine that the theological focus you've chosen will be the theme in your youth ministry for a month. What are some ways you'll get the concept across? What biblical anchoring will you use?

Competencies in Youth Ministry:
What You Ought to Know, Be, or Do in Order to Be an Effective Youth Pastor

Allan Jackson, Ph.D.

Associate Professor of Youth Education, New Orleans Baptist Theological Seminary

My son got a speedometer for his bicycle this Christmas. Naturally, it came in a box, with instructions printed in several different languages. I got my tools out and promised him that he would have a measurement for his need for speed in no time—Dad was on the job. Two hours later, I gave up. I pronounced the speedometer "defective" (a time-honored word used when a dad cannot figure out how to assemble said toy) and told my wife to return it to the store.

My wife asked me if I had read the instructions. I told her that I had, mostly. She asked me if it had batteries, and I said it did. She asked me if I would call Nick, the nice young man at the sports superstore, to discuss the problem. I said I wouldn't. I did say that I would be glad to load the bicycle into the car and she could go see Nick in the bicycle department to let him verify my diagnosis that the thing was broken. It took Nick all of about five minutes to discern that I had installed the magnet upside down. My new diagnosis was that I was an idiot.

Nick is much younger than I am. He has about twelve fewer years of school than I do. He has not traveled, he does not get invited to speak, he has not written any books. But he knows how to fix bicycles. He has the knowledge concerning bicycle accessories, and he has the confidence that he can repair what fathers destroy, and he has acquired the skills necessary to work on bicycles.

He has competency as a bicycle technician.

The phone call came unexpectedly. "Gary, you need to know that we love you as a person and we think you are going to develop into a fine youth pastor. It's just that right now, you do not seem to be ready for the youth ministry at our church."

With the one-sided conversation from the personnel team, a young student minister was without a place to serve. The reason given was that he was "overmatched" or that he was "not quite ready." The perception among people at the church was that Gary lacked something that he should have in order to do effective youth ministry.

Gary has the Bible college degree. He has experience in a smaller church. He is a pretty good youth communicator. He has every available volume in the Ideas library, and most importantly, he has passion to help students be in relationship with Jesus Christ. What is lacking? Why has Gary moved to another church?

He is perceived to lack competencies needed to be a youth pastor at this particular church.

It could be a skill, or an ability, or a personality trait, or a good chemistry with the senior pastor. It could be experience or administrative ability, or maturity or charisma. Whatever is perceived to be lacking, and what cost him his job, could be viewed as a competency.

As youth ministry moves deeper into the 21st century, it is not much of a stretch to say that youth ministry has become more complex. A youth pastor needs to have understanding, if not expertise, in any number of areas that were not considered part of the job even 25-30 years ago. Risk management, Internet accountability, time management in an age of instant accessibility—these and more were not part of the bag of tricks back in the old days. More competency in a greater number of categories is needed to survive and thrive in youth ministry today.

"Competent" is defined as "having requisite or adequate ability or qualities." In layman's terms, that means that a person has the necessary set of knowledge, skills, and attitudes to accomplish a task or do a job. Competent can also be applied in a legal sense as in, "competent to stand trial," or "competent as a witness," meaning that from the standpoint of the law, the testimony given in court is reliable because it comes from someone who knows what he/she is doing.

"Competency" is a noun form of "competent" and is used to describe a particular knowledge, skill, or attitude needed to do a job (i.e., theology) or some combination of knowledge, skill, or attitude (i.e., time management) needed to do a job. Let's say that Bridget, a youth minister at the First Church of Perpetual Motion, could be described as having a competency in "ropes course leadership." I would assume that she would have these attributes:

- The knowledge required—safety procedures, purpose of high and low elements, understanding of how the element is to be accomplished, debriefing information, and so on.

- The skills required—ability to belay, agility to model the procedure to be used for each element, ability to react to potentially dangerous "surprises," basic first aid, ability to debrief each element so that students can tie a lesson to the activity, et cetera.

- The attitude required—passion for adventure recreation, genuine love for the persons who will participate, excitement concerning the "fun factor" of high ropes, thrill to see a teenager "get it" regarding the connection between ropes and spiritual application, and so on.

Competencies for youth ministry

What would be the competency set needed for leading a youth ministry or being a youth pastor? Some important voices have been talking about competencies which may be specialized for youth ministers. Rick Dunn indicated that there are unique skills and abilities necessary for effective youth ministry. Dave Rahn suggested that youth ministers share competencies with other ministers in the area of Christian maturity, but need special skills in the area of understanding the nature of youth ministry. Rahn called for research to identify the list of things that every youth minister, regardless of specialty, ought to learn.

Mark Senter, writing in *Reaching a Generation for Christ*, indicated that the starting point for a discussion of youth ministry competencies is the false presupposition that youth ministers are "...young, male, musically talented, charismatic, entertaining, and culturally relevant in appearance." Senter challenged the stereotypical description by suggesting that regardless of the age, gender, musical talent, enthusiasm, or relevance of a youth pastor (or presumably in the absence of a paid youth pastor), a number of assumptions set the stage for effective youth ministry. He called the assumptions "axioms."

- Axiom 1: Youth ministry begins when a Christian adult finds a comfortable method of entering a student's world.
- Axiom 2: Youth ministry happens as long as a Christian adult is able to use his or her contact with a student to draw that student into a maturing relationship with God through Jesus Christ.
- Axiom 3: Youth ministry ceases to take place when the adult-student relationship is broken or no longer moves the student toward spiritual maturity.
- Axiom 4: The influence of the student's family on his or her value system will exceed the influence of the youth worker on most occasions.
- Axiom 5: When everything else is said and done, the role of the Christian youth group is to pass biblical values from one generation to the next.
- Axiom 6: Youth ministry prospers where the Bible is taken seriously and is used as the basis for faith and life.
- Axiom 7: A youth ministry will reflect the vision of its adult leaders.

With the assumptions as foundational, the role of the youth minister is the next building block. This person, paid or volunteer, feels personally responsible for the youth ministry, and is authorized by the church or ministry to plan, implement, and evaluate the youth ministry program. That person's calling, character, and competence will shape much of the church's work with teenagers. Every parish-based (local church) youth ministry needs the following:

- Someone who sees the big picture
- Someone to build motivation
- Someone to relate to other staff, elders, or church governing body
- Someone to plan and administer the budget

- Someone to give visibility to the church's work with youth
- Someone to coordinate the youth calendar, including special events as well as the weekly youth program
- Someone to take the lead in enlisting and training other adults to serve with youth

(Time out: these "lists" are looking like job descriptions. In a way, they are. A church or parachurch ministry should consider axioms and youth ministry needs before a person is ever sought or hired to be the youth pastor. Just as a church needs to think through the foundation of youth ministry before calling a youth pastor, so a potential youth pastor brings a set of assumptions to any youth ministry position, regardless of the setting. It is assumed that a youth minister should aspire to and have a sense of confidence that he or she can do these things.)

- Grow spiritually—one cannot lead where one does not go.

- Lead ministries that lead students to Christ—ultimately, what makes it ministry is the desire to see non-Christian kids find a relationship with Jesus.

- Lead ministries that make disciples and disciple-makers—Jesus modeled that we are to equip students to spiritually reproduce.

- Attend to the details of day-to-day youth ministry—administration keeps youth ministers organized and employed.

My job as a teacher of youth ministry at a seminary gets at the heart of that question—what do I need to teach youth pastors in seminary? Even more pointed is the question, "Can I actually teach everything or anything that will help a youth pastor succeed in leading an effective youth ministry in a local church or parachurch setting?" Anyone who seeks to equip youth pastors, whether it is in a seminary classroom or at a Youth Specialties convention, is trying to identify the set of knowledge, skill, and attitude necessary to lead effective youth ministry in today's cultural context.

In an age of "purpose driven-ness," it would make sense that those of us who attempt to train youth pastors would be purposeful about our task. Each course, and each assignment in these courses, should be intentional in helping youth pastors acquire the knowledge, learn the skills, and sharpen the attitudes which will help them to be successful in carrying out their calling in a local setting. To that end, our team at the Youth Ministry Institute has been reading, asking questions, and listening to youth pastors tell us what competencies a) they are glad they have or b) they wish they had. I will simply give it to you in a list and let you make your own applications.

Competency 1: Personal skills
- Be able to articulate with clarity one's call to ministry.
- Perceive self as a part of the ministry team who leads the faith community.

- Work effectively with and through the church staff.
- Develop and consistently implement a Christian work ethic.
- Develop confidence to equip and supervise volunteers and interns.
- Be aware of and implement a strategy for reducing personal and ministry-related risk—the temptation to engage in private sin is greater (and easier) than ever before.
- See the need for and be able to stay refreshed spiritually.
- Understand and interpret the youth culture, both locally and globally.
- Implement personal time management strategies

Competency 2: People Skills

- Interact effectively with senior pastor and other staff members.
- Build relationships with teenagers, parents, and youth leaders, and help teenagers build relationships with their peers, their families, and their leaders.
- Provide short-term counseling for teenagers and adults, and understand the processes of helping individuals and groups in crisis, including referral.
- Develop a strategy for discipline in the youth ministry.
- Help youth leaders and teenagers develop coping skills.

Competency 3: Administration

- Develop and articulate a vision for youth ministry in the local church.
- Discern needs among youth in their church region in order to direct relevant ministry.
- Design and implement need-based, ongoing educational programming which, through adult volunteers, addresses the basic functions of the church, including discipleship, ministry, worship, evangelism, and fellowship.
- Provide competent administration in youth ministry activities, programs, and budgeting.

Competency 4: Leadership

- Lead strategic planning and coordinate the structures through which to implement the vision.
- Enlist, train, and encourage adult volunteers in their ministries with teenagers.
- Provide ongoing leadership development (both training and opportunity to lead).
- Instruct in the discipleship and disciple-making process.

Competency 5: Biblical, theological, pastoral

- Study and interpret the Scripture using various study tools.
- Communicate scriptural truth in large and small groups.

• Embrace and articulate right doctrine and intimacy with Christ as part of vision and strategy.
• Appreciate and demonstrate the urgency of pastoral care in the youth ministry.

While we are seeking to identify specific competencies in order to be more intentional about training, we shouldn't get caught up in the academic-sounding language. Youth ministry is still about relationships. We desire to build ministry in people that will last if we should leave. We wish to "do justice, love mercy, and walk humbly with our God." And because we want to make a difference in our church, community, and for the kingdom, the need to identify and acquire competence is greater than ever before.

For Reflection and Discussion

Look back through the list of skills: personal (1-9), people (10-14), administrative (15-18), leadership (19-22), and biblical (23-26).

1) From your own experience in youth ministry as a teenager or your involvement in ministry now, try to come up with a good or bad example from each of the five competencies of Dr. Jackson's list.

2) Go back through the list, 1-26. Which one in each of the five categories are you strongest in? In which do you need the most growth?

How Your Personality Affects Your Ministry

Len Kageler, Ph.D.
Professor of Youth Ministry, Youth Ministry Chair, Nyack College

AN AUTOBIOGRAPHICAL CASE STUDY:

After the interview process and weeks of discussion and prayer, a church foot the bill to move my family (wife, three daughters) and me 3000 miles across the country so I could be their youth pastor. They also agreed to pay me a humongous salary, about double the already pretty good income I was making at the church I left. Two things helped that church feel "we gotta have this guy." First, I was able to articulate what I was good at. Secondly, I was able to explain to them how I would help their volunteer staff be encouraged, equipped, and unleashed to serve God with enthusiastic joy. And, for the most part, I was able to do that because I had some sense of the strengths and weaknesses of my own personality. It's an area of self-awareness that is very helpful.

Hippocrates and youth ministry

Personality differences have been a subject of curiosity and speculation for millennia. Hippocrates began the labeling process 2,500 years ago, and today, personality theory receives much academic attention. A few decades ago it was fashionable to understand personality differences as simply the result of upbringing and environment. To a large extent, those notions have been jettisoned.

What is currently understood about personality can be summarized as follows:

1. Personality differences can almost entirely be explained by genetics.

2. People who understand their personality and how it affects and interacts with others are much more prone to "success" in life when it comes to relationships, career, and money.

Christians can be quite comfortable with especially the first of these statements. After all, we believe we were created. And why wouldn't God want people to be different? One doesn't have to be a theologian to understand that each person is to have a different function in the Body of Christ. The teaching of Scripture on spiritual gifts is clear about this (see Ephesians 4, 1 Corinthians 12, and Romans 12). Biblically we understand that no one individual has "all the gifts" and that people must be in community, or on a team, for the fullest expression of all what God wants to do in, among, and through his people.

Understanding Your Personality

There are many personality inventories and conceptual frameworks in the lexicon of personality differences. Among the most popular are the Myers-Briggs Type Indicator and IDAK.

My favorite way of understanding personality differences is by using the terms introduced by Smalley and Trent in *The Two Sides of Love: Lions, Otters, Golden Retrievers, and Beavers*.

- Lions are leaders and can be aggressive. They like to make decisions and make things happen.
- Otters are the life-of-the-party, fun-loving, people-persons who love to have wide social contacts.
- Golden Retrievers are deeply relational and sensitive. They love to get inside the head and heart of another person.
- Beavers love to be factual, organized, and analytical. They make decisions comfortably only when they have as much factual information as possible.

To better understand these four "animals," though, let's first imagine four different rooms.

Let's walk into a room full of Beavers. It's a quiet room, but happy. Beavers don't require a lot of social interaction. Some Beavers will be talking quietly and seriously; others will be saying nothing at all; and some Beavers will have brought a book or notebook computer along to make the best use of their time. Beavers are quite content without a party.

Now come into a room full of Golden Retrievers. The noise level is slightly higher here because Golden Retrievers love to talk, and talk deeply. They are sharing, listening, and are very focused. If the building were on fire, those in the Golden Retriever room might not hear the alarm to begin with, but if they did, they would be hesitant to go until a natural break occurred in the deep conversation.

If you dare, come into a room full of Otters. It's party time! In this room people are laughing, joking around, and clearly enjoying one another. Paper airplanes sail across the room and (look out!) someone brought a squirt gun. Otters love action and would rather not be alone. Otters feel responsible to help everyone have a good time.

Let's go now to the only room I hesitate to show you. It is the only unhappy room of the four. You see, Lions are uncomfortable until they figure out which of them is the top Lion. Until that is sorted out, there can be some terse exchanges, one-upmanship talk, and verbal sparring to see who gets the high ground.

"Lions, Otters, and Beavers, Oh My!"

It's not hard to see how these four personality types differ when it comes to job satisfaction. Lions are happiest when in charge of something or someone. They like to manage and give orders; making decisions is "no problemo." Otters make great salespeople; they love jobs where the expectation is to gain instant rapport and make people happy. Don't put an Otter behind a desk for long, because she or he will want to be out and about with people. Golden Retrievers make great customer service representatives or any job where the key is to convey care. Some years ago I had a new Ford Taurus and had a persistent and recurring problem that continued after the warranty period was long gone. I called Ford customer service, and it was clearly a Golden Retriever on the other end. She listened, acknowledged my pain, and said that hell would freeze over before Ford would do anything for me. No, those were not her exact words, but that was the gist of what she conveyed to me. And you know what? I didn't feel that bad afterward, because most of all, someone listened to my pain. Listening to another's pain is what Golden Retrievers are born to do. Beavers make great accountants, actuaries, and programmers. Facing a day of minimal human contact is no problem to them! It's energizing, not draining.

Good News for All Types

It is encouraging to know that God uses all kinds of people in youth work. His calling is not limited to any one type. If we think about Jesus' selection of the Twelve, we are reminded that he chose a variety of personalities who would eventually be let loose to turn the world upside down.

Let's consider the strengths of each personality type as it pertains to youth ministry. Here we get at the heart of how your personality will affect your own youth ministry.

Lions

Lions have no hesitation about standing up in front of the troops. To lead a youth ministry someone has to be up there, right? If not a Lion adult, then a Lion kid can be comfortable being in charge. Many people fear speaking in public more than they fear death itself. But guess what? Lions do not have this problem. They are great at providing directions, vision, and a sense that this youth ministry is going places. They don't get bogged down with decision-making. They make those decisions and then "go for it."

There is much in a Lion that is attractive to teenagers. Kids like a sense of purpose and direction. They want meaning. Lions are great when it comes to speaking and leading youth into meaningful challenges.

Otters

In my office library I have a 500-page text titled *The Sociology of Leisure*. Well, Otters don't need a book to understand fun! Otters want to have a good time, but their desire is not selfish. They want others to have a good time as well. In youth work, Otters are the kind of people who make kids smile, laugh, and go home exclaiming, "That was awesome!" Otters are into fun, be it a spontaneous trip to Pizza Hut or a long-planned Jello-wrestling outreach event.

Otters make great youth workers because they want to make sure every single kid who walks in the door feels at least a little bit good. Otters work hard to create a positive atmosphere that attracts youths and makes them feel comfortable. Kids are attracted to Otters because they're attracted to life. An Otter-led youth ministry is one in which youths feel good about the group and their involvement in it. They enjoy bringing friends because they know their friends will have a good time and hear a positive message.

Golden Retrievers

Youth work is a job made in heaven for Golden Retrievers. Adolescence is a stormy time and it is rare when a kid doesn't feel insecure or hurting about something. Golden Retrievers are there for them! The gift of time and the gift of listening are blessings that Golden Retrievers bring to a youth ministry. They are concerned that the personal needs of young people be met.

Golden Retrievers are especially good at hanging out before and after a meeting or event. I have seen kids and Golden Retrievers standing around just talking in the parking lot long after the youth room is cleaned up and the lights are turned off. Kids are attracted to Golden Retriever-led youth groups because they know they've got a friend. Programs do not bring people; people bring people. The connectedness kids feel to the Golden Retrievers in a youth group ensure their return again and again.

Beavers

Beavers can make great youth workers too. Some kids are Beavers and they can immediately sense when the leader is one of their own. Beavers are never sloppy in their organization of the ministry. Kids and parents know that if it appears on the youth calendar, it is going to happen and all the details will be covered. The event, the ministry, is going to flow because the myriad of details needed to run a youth ministry are both understood and handled eagerly by Beavers. Beavers keep people informed, they don't lose money, and their word is good.

Kids like Beavers because they like stability, trustworthiness, and excellence. Many appreciate the one-on-one emphasis which is all too absent in many homes.

While each personality type drips with potential for excellent youth ministry, there is, unfortunately, a downside to every upside. Our personalities, with all their God-given strengths, also have weaknesses.

Lions can be insensitive and pushy, cause people to feel their opinions don't matter, and make rash decisions. Otters tend to be disorganized, last-minute in preparation, and lacking in follow-through (especially in little details). Golden Retrievers have a hard time standing in front of more than 15 energetic middle schoolers. Beavers won't attract many Otter youths since they find it difficult to project enthusiasm in the group setting.

Go Beyond Understanding—Become One Who Unleashes

We take a big step when we understand and maximize the strengths of our personality. We take another huge step when we understand our role in youth ministry is helping volunteer staff figure out their own personalities. Get the Smalley and Trent book, and let your staff take the personality test. Have them talk about how they see the truth in what they've just discovered.

Once everyone knows everyone's personality, let 'em loose! Remember the church that paid "top dollar" for me to come? Here's what their volunteer staff understood after the group interview:

I was a Lion/Otter. They could see my understanding of them and what it would mean if I was their youth pastor:

The Lions would sometimes be in charge of programs and projects. They would get their chance to be in front of the group, as well as make decisions.

The Otters knew the ministry wouldn't be boring. They saw a fellow Otter. They understood the ministry would be fun not only for the kids, but the staff as well.

The Golden Retrievers breathed sighs of relief because I freely acknowledged my weakness in personal caring and counseling. They understood I would want the kids to come to them with their pain and I would not be jealous of the deep relationships they had with kids.

The Beavers were happy because I was a fairly organized Lion, but I affirmed and acknowledged the ministry's need for their strengths in things like one-to-one mentoring, keeping track of fund-raising monies, detail planning for events, et cetera.

"The Otter Cannot Say To the Lion, 'I Don't Need You'"

God made each of us wonderfully and uniquely. There is amazing joy in knowing what we're good at and getting to do it. There is amazing joy as well in seeing people come alive in ministry because they understand the personality strengths with which they've been blessed.

For Reflection and Discussion

1) So, which are you (Lion, Otter, Golden Retriever, or Beaver)? Give examples illustrating your choice.

2) As you think about your youth ministry experience (past or present), have you ever seen or experienced the downside of a particular personality? For example, a youth leader who was outgoing and really fun but also really disorganized and perhaps even reckless?

Beyond Kitchens and Kool-Aid:
A Theological Look at Women in Youth Ministry

Helen Musick
Instructor in Youth Ministry, Asbury Theological Seminary;
and Karen Thomas

Billy's mother dreaded telling her four-year-old son that Pastor Smith was leaving their small, rural church. Even at a young age, Billy had grown fond of his pastor, who had served the church since before Billy's birth. Denominational leadership had decided to move the pastor to a new congregation miles from Billy's town.

Gently lifting Billy onto her lap, she said, "Billy, I have something to tell you. I know that Pastor Smith has been very special to you. I know you love to walk to the front of the church and listen to the children's sermon each Sunday." She paused, "But Pastor Smith is moving to a new church. This is her last Sunday."

Billy's eyes lost their sparkle. Holding back tears, he replied, "Why, Mommy? I love Pastor Smith. She is so nice. She always gives me a hug after the story."

Billy's mom tried hard to articulate the denomination's decision so that this precious little boy could understand. "Billy, Pastor Smith must help another group of children learn about Jesus." Trying to restore some of his joy, she continued, "But Billy, you are going to have a new pastor. His name is Pastor Bob. He is a very nice man."

Billy's face switched from sadness to bewilderment. He cried, "You mean our new pastor is a man?"

"Yes, dear," replied his mother.

"But Mommy," Billy replied with a sense of certainty, "Men can't be pastors!"

In a ministry culture where the leaders are predominantly male, this true story evokes a chuckle. Most people today approach gender roles for ministers much differently than Billy did. Confusion abounds. "A woman pastor? Women can't be pastors!"

As Jesus ascended into heaven, he declared, "All authority in heaven and on earth has been given to me. Therefore go and make disciples of all nations, baptizing them in the name of the Father and of the Son and of the Holy Spirit" (Matt. 28:18-19). The Great Commission has been proclaimed from pulpits and street corners for centuries.

Ironically, a woman who seeks to obey Christ and his commission may find herself in direct opposition to many church denominations' rules of order. Historically, a woman can "make disciples" of children and other women, but not men. And what a heresy if she would even think of baptizing someone! Should we assume that the Great Commission was only a command for men? Must the church differentiate between decrees given to men and decrees given to women? How can church bureaucracy deny women the opportunity to minister when Paul specifically states that in Christ, "There is neither Jew nor Greek, slave nor free, male nor female, for you are all one in Christ Jesus"? (Gal. 3:28)

The debate concerning women in ministry has raged since the birth of the church. In fact, many leading historical theologians' and philosophers' views of women were downright degrading. Aristotle believed that a woman was a "mutilated male" who lacked the substance of soul. Thomas Aquinas noted that women's individual natures were "defective and misbegotten." Immanuel Kant said, " She does not possess certain high insights, she is timid, and not fit for serious employments." The Roman Catholic position prior to the Reformation asserted, "Women are unclean pawns of the devil who lure men to sins of lust." Utilizing Scripture, Martin Luther and John Calvin argued that "both men and women were created in the image of God and therefore stood before God as equals." However, neither Reformer supported women in actual church ministry. Centuries later, the Puritans, Quakers, and Methodists did begin to allow women to preach and teach. Overall, however, women have been banished to the nursery, Sunday School classrooms, or the foreign mission field. Ruth Tucker states, "The debate over women in ministry is really a debate over women and authority. No one argues that women should not have ministry. They may not, however, perform ministry that entails authority—so argues the traditionalist."

When studying Scripture in its entirety, we can't help but notice God's high value of women, and their equality with males. Jesus' affirming actions toward women were revolutionary in his culture. When Scripture speaks of spiritual gifts, unity and oneness in Christ are emphasized. Gifts are never designated specifically to males or females. Yet, in the work of the church, women are often oppressed and marginalized in such areas as preaching, teaching, administration, prophecy, and apostleship.

As Scripture is the ultimate truth and at the heart of this debate, the focus here is on biblical texts. We must remember that the Word of God holds authority over human opinion. From the outset, it must be noted that biblical scholars tend to agree that the passages on women in the church challenge their scholarly exegesis. Godly men and women stand on opposing sides of this argument.

Creation and Curse

The creation account of humanity is the starting point of any discussion concerning gender roles. We must remember that both man and woman were created equal. "In the image of God" who thought it was "very good" (Gen.1). This scriptural teaching directly opposed the surrounding culture in which kings were the only ones believed to possess "images of God."

Many fundamentalists point back to the creation to establish the precedent for relational order. James Hurley notes, "Christian worship involves re-establishing the creational pattern with men faithfully teaching God's truth and women receptively listening." However, there is no basis for this position in Genesis. Sexual hierarchy did not exist. Man and woman lived in perfect harmony and democracy. Adam stated, "This is now bone of my bones and flesh of my flesh" (Gen. 2:23). Whenever "bone of my bones" appears in the Hebrew Bible it means kinship or similarity, never subordination. The ancient Greeks believed that women were made of inferior material compared to men. Scripture, however, states that women and men were made of the same flesh. Others argue that the male is the superior sex because Adam was created before Eve. This concept is not substantiated, as the order of creation does not grant advantage. After all, the animals were created before man.

Unfortunately, church fathers often took the position that women only possessed the image of God in relation to their husbands. St. Augustine taught, "When she is assigned as a helpmate, a function that pertains to her alone, then she is not the image of God; but as far as the man is concerned, he is by himself the image of God." In the English language, one may think of a "helper" as a subordinate servant, yet the Hebrew word for helper, *ezer*, refers to strength. Noted 21 times in the Old Testament, *ezer* is used mostly in relation to God as mighty helper. The term never implies subordination.

Women have often been the "scapegoats" for the fall of humanity. Concerning women, Tertullian wrote, "You are the devil's gateway; you are the unsealer of that tree; you are the first deserter of the divine law; you are she who persuaded him who the devil was not valiant enough to attack. You destroyed so easily God's image, man." Interestingly, in Genesis 2:16-17 God addresses Adam in the plural form of "you," possibly indicating that he is speaking to both Adam and Eve. Also, there is not mention of Adam's protest to Eve's action. He also readily eats the fruit.

The fact remains today that all creation suffers the effects of the fall, regardless of blame being placed. The curse upon the female gender is that "your desire shall be for your husband, and he shall rule over you" (Gen. 3:16, NASB). Because Eve overstepped her bounds, now women are naturally plagued with the problem of social dominance. Phyllis Tribble asserts that this curse describes role relationships; it does not prescribe male dominance. The tense of "he shall rule" is future tense and is used as a prediction of prophecy, not a command.

Jesus ended the curse by taking it upon himself for humanity. He was born into a world where women were believed to be inferior, yet he allowed them to travel with him. He praised Mary for sitting at his feet as theological student. He abolished double standards in adultery and divorce. Instead of blaming women for male lust, he blamed men themselves. In a society where women could not even testify in a court of law, Jesus chose them to be the first to witness his resurrection.

Women and men were created equal, as partners, and helpers. The fall cursed and skewed their relationship, as demonstrated by the extremely patriarchal culture of the old covenant. The reign of Christ, however, reverses the curse and allows equality to reign once again.

Women in the Bible

Noted biblical egalitarian Faith Martin states, "In the patriarchy, the power of the male over females was direct, personal, and absolute. In each stage of her life, a woman was under the civil authority of a specific man—first her father, then her husband, and, if she was widowed, her son... All males were permanent family members; they had rights, privileges, and future power within the family...Women passed from one family to another, never owning property." From the Old Testament, we learn that women were often used and abused, especially in polygamy. Ceremonial laws were more stringent for females, especially concerning uncleanness and a female's menstruation cycle. Martin asserts that women may not have been priests simply because there were so many days each month, even more if they were pregnant, that they could not appear before the Lord.

Despite the obstacles against women, God powerfully used many women in the salvation history of Israel. Two Old Testament books are named after women. Ruth was the great-grandmother of King David, and Esther saved the nation of Israel. At least five women prophetesses are mentioned in the Old Testament: Miriam, Deborah, Huldah, Noadiah, and the unnamed mother of Isaiah. Deborah was not only a prophetess, she was also a judge and a military leader. Gilbert Bilezikian makes an interesting point when he says, "Abraham is shown as obeying Sarah as often as Sarah obeyed Abraham."

Throughout the New Testament, women were at Jesus' side as they ministered to him and to others. Phoebe and Priscilla performed administrative and ministerial duties with Paul. In Romans 16, Phoebe is a diakonos, which is translated "servant." Interestingly, whenever the same word is used with a man's name, it is translated "deacon" or "minister."

Other noted women in Christian leadership in the first century church include Lydia, Chloe, Euodia and Syntyche, Mary, Trypaena, Persis, Eunice, Nympha, and Appia. Philip's four daughters were prophetesses. Eight women are listed in Paul's concluding words in Romans 16. Paul sanctioned women to be deacons (Rom 16:1), helpers (Rom. 16:2), fellow workers (Rom. 16:3; Phil. 4:2ff), prophets (1 Cor. 11:5), teachers (Titus 2:3), apostles (Rom. 16:7), and possibly also elders (1 Tim. 5:2).

Christian apologist Dorothy Sayers' comments concerning Jesus are worth noting:

"Perhaps it is no wonder that the women were first at the cradle and last at the cross. They had never known a man like this man—there never has been such another. A Prophet and teacher who never nagged at them, never flattered or coaxed or patronized; who never made arch jokes about them, never treated them as "The women, God help us!" or "The ladies, God bless them!"; who rebuked without garrulousness and praised without condescension; who never mapped out their sphere for them, never urged them to be feminine or jeered at them for being female; who had no ax to grind and no uneasy male dignity to defend; who took them as he found them and was completely unself-conscious."

Paul's Problematic Passages

There are passages in the New Testament that raise questions: "Women should remain silent in the churches," and "I do not permit a woman to teach or have authority over a man." These two statements of Paul's writing, as well as others, are often used to stop women from exercising all of their spiritual gifts. If silence and banning women from teaching are the true intent of these Scriptures, then we immediately bow in obedience to the Word of God. However, in all quality biblical hermeneutics, the context must rule the interpretation. Should women still wear head coverings? Am I in sin wearing jewelry? These particular passages have been interpreted in light of context and culture. Paul's passages must also be examined in their contextual fullness.

Dr. M. Robert Mulholland has presented new insights into the Pauline dilemma. He purports that two different paradigms are aligned in Paul's epistles, specifically women relating to men, and wives relating to husbands, noting that the failure to discern these two very different and distinct frames of reference in discussing the roles and relationships of men and women is a major contributor to the apparent discrepancy of the Biblical witness and to the often polarized debate over the role of women in the church.

Paul's linguistics delineate the two different paradigms. He always uses the term *gyne* for women and wives; yet he uses *anthropos* for men and *aner* for husbands. Of the 57 uses of *aner* in the New Testament, all except four are used solely for husband, and 15 are used in the problematic passages. Mulholland's thesis will be used as a backdrop to examine each of the passages.

1 Corinthians 14:34-35:

"Women should remain silent in the churches. They are not allowed to speak, but must be in submission, as the Law says. If they want to inquire about something, they should ask their own husbands at home, for it is disgraceful for a woman to speak in church."

First, one must realize that Paul is addressing wives in this passage, urging them to address questions to their husbands in private. In the broader context, this was the third group that Paul silenced. In 14:28, Paul silenced those speaking in tongues if no interpreter was available. In 14:29, Paul silenced the prophets so that others could gain revelation. Then, Paul silenced the wives. The problem rested in women capitalizing on their new equality in Christ to initiate issues that should be discussed within the marital relationship. Furthermore, the statement, "it is disgraceful for a woman to speak in church," focuses on marital troubles; Paul, in 11:5, had already fully sanctioned women in public prayer and prophesy.

Furthermore, the church at Corinth experienced chaos in worship. Paul addressed this dilemma, desiring that all would share in exercising their spiritual gifts in an orderly manner. Composed of converted pagans, the Corinthian church needed to continually distinguish itself from the surrounding pagan cults. The pagan women's cults were marked by wild, out-of-control behavior. Some scholars believe these verses silenced "specific uncontrolled babbling (sacred cries—*lalao*) of newly-converted Gentile women." Most scholars believe that this was a "limited prohibition." Jews and Gentiles separated the males and females in worship, yet the Christian church introduced worship together. It is probable that some took this freedom beyond its intended limits.

1 Timothy 2:12-15:

"I do not permit woman to teach or to have authority over a man; she must be silent. For Adam was formed first, then Eve. And Adam was not the one deceived; it was the woman who was deceived and became a sinner. But women will be saved through childbearing—if they continue in faith, love and holiness with propriety."

Linguistically, one must note that the tense of the verb "to permit" is present, indicating a temporary prohibition, not one that is binding for all time. The normal Greek word for authority is *exousia*. However, the word *authentein* is translated "have authority" in this passage and is only used once in the New Testament. Thus, scholars utilized extrabiblical sources to determine the meaning of "to usurp authority" or "to domineer over." Keyes states, "All of the possible meanings indicated negative, abusive and illegitimate actions or attitudes." The message is not that women should have no authority over men, but that they should not abuse, domineer, or usurp authority.

One may feel offended if commanded to learn in silence today, because our society values interaction. Yet in Paul's era, sitting in silence under a rabbi was normal. Almost unbelievable to Paul's culture was the desire for women to learn! Aida Spencer states, "Silence was...a positive attribute for rabbinic students. Paul's words were declaring to his Jewish friends that at this time, women were to be learning in the same manner as did rabbinic students."

The pastoral epistles focus on the theme of heresy and false teaching. One third of I Timothy addresses the heresies that were filling the church. Women in the church were propagating Gnosticism, which condemned matter and elevated the spirit and knowledge. They believed that they were receiving special messages from God. Biblical scholars Richard and Catherine Kroeger state, "Ephesus... has been called the bastion of the female spiritual principle in ancient religion. Remember that the group claimed for their prophetesses a special revelation, superior to that afforded to men, and even to Christ." The women speaking out of order were unorthodox heretics who sought to usurp authority with their special revelation. Paul does not prohibit orthodox female teachers, as he notes Priscilla's influence on Apollos and Eunice and Lois' influence on Timothy.

Creating myths and genealogies was a favorite Gnostic pastime, with the creation story as their specialty. Often, they would reorder creation to place woman first in the creation order and impart wisdom to Adam. Understandably, one sees why Paul must recount the creation narrative in 1 Timothy. Furthermore, Gnostics also believed that women should strive to become like men, denying marriage and childbearing. In so doing, good spirits would no longer have residence in evil flesh. Paul was refuting this teaching and elevating femininity in 1 Timothy 2:15. Women, like men, are saved by grace through faith in Christ Jesus alone.

Another problem passage is found in 1 Timothy 3 where Paul lists the qualifications of an overseer. First, one must note, if one holds this literally, it also rules out all single men, like Paul and Jesus. Polygamy was a common practice among Jewish and Gentile men. Women did not participate. Thus the exhortation, "the husband of but one wife," was necessary.

1 Corinthians 11:3-12:

"Now I want you to realize that the head of every man is Christ, and the head of the woman is man, and the head of Christ is God... And every woman who prays or prophesies with her head uncovered dishonors her head...the woman is the glory of man. For man did not come from woman, but woman came from man...In the Lord, however, woman is not independent of man, nor is man independent of woman. For as woman came from man, so also man is born of woman. But everything comes from God."

Scholars admit that this is one of the most difficult passages to interpret in the entire corpus of Scripture. In the Greek, man is *aner*, signifying that the passage focuses on husbands and wives, not men and women in a church setting. Furthermore, a "veil" in the Roman-Hellenistic world was worn by married women to signify their unavailability. The word for "head" in Greek is *kephale*, which does not mean "authority," but "source" or "origin." Contextually, this agrees as the passage concludes with "everything comes from God." Traditionalists view the "head" concept as one of rulership and domination. The body submits to the thoughts and actions of the head.

However, Fred Layman contests this concept. He states, "To begin with, the function of the head (brain) in rational processes was not known prior to the rise of modern science. The ancients didn't have the remotest idea of the function of the brain and the nervous system and attributed psychical functions to the soul, the spirit, or to other parts of the body—the heart, the bowels, the kidneys, the bones, etc.—but never the head." The headship of Christ to the church is seen as self-sacrificing, cherishing, and nurturing. The relationship of mutual submission between husband and wife was revolutionary to the culture. In Christ, the curse of male domination and female subordination was broken. Freedom was restored for all.

Women Leaders in Church History

Beyond Scripture, there have been many women in leadership positions within the church. Noted Christian historian Philip Schaff writes, "It should not be forgotten that many virgins of the early church devoted their whole energies to the care for the sick and the poor, or exhibited as martyrs a degree of passive virtue and moral heroism altogether unknown before." Vibia Perpetua was one of the most well-known early female martyrs in North Africa. The monastic life provided opportunities for many women to exercise their faith and charity. The Reformation ushered in a new biblical view of women, yet did nothing to alter their status within the church.

Women found freedom in almost every sectarian movement following the Reformation. Women were given equal status in the Quaker church from its inception. John and Charles Wesley's mother, Susanna, was noted as a "preacher of righteousness." Catherine Booth cofounded the Salvation Army alongside her husband. Clarissa Danforth preached at revivals throughout New England in the nineteenth century. Jerena Lee, a black revival minister with the African Episcopal Church, led many to saving faith. Evangelist Maggie Van Cott was often compared to Dwight L. Moody, bringing thousands to faith each year. The most well-known female evangelist of the nineteenth century was Phoebe Palmer, "Mother of the Holiness Movement." She traveled internationally, with an estimated 25,000 conversions.

The mission field opened wide to women as church denominations realized the need was greater than the "man" power available. Tucker states, "Few of these mission leaders even contemplated the inconsistency of denying women ministry in their own homeland while encouraging such ministry abroad." Unfortunately, some missions which were once open to women are now closed.

The Call and Commission

To go back to our opening story, Billy thinks that only women can be pastors. Is that fair to men? Many think only men can be pastors. Is that fair to women? We know that

Scripture supports the equal distribution of gifts and the call to obedience in using them. The command to "Go and make disciples" is a universal call for both males and females. The prophetic words of Joel, which Peter declared fulfilled on the day of Pentecost, remind us of this. "In the last days, God says, I will pour out My Spirit on all people. Your sons and daughters will prophesy, your young men will see visions, your old men will dream dreams. Even on My servants, *both men and women*, I will pour out My spirit in those days, and they will prophesy" (Acts 2:17, 18, emphasis added).

Both of us [Helen and Karen] grew up in Protestant homes with religious parents who were committed to teaching us the ways of Christ. However, neither one of us was exposed to women in full-time ministry until we reached our twenties. We both wonder how our lives would have been different if we had had a female youth pastor or mentor earlier in our lives.

The body of Christ is crying out for women leaders who desire to minister faithfully with the talents God has given them. Youth today need positive role models of both genders for healthy relational development and deep understanding of the call of Christ. Speaking of the servant who did nothing with the talents given, Jesus declared, "You wicked, lazy servant!" (Matt. 25:26)

May each of us faithfully and unashamedly walk out the call and commission placed on our lives, praying fervently that we will one day hear Jesus say, "Well done, good and faithful servant!"

For Reflection and Discussion

1) Have you been in a church or situation where women in ministry was a controversy? If so, to what extent did you find opposing sides listening to each other? What can you learn for future conflict situations, for better or worse, from your observation of the women in ministry controversy?

2) What is your position on women in ministry? If you do not agree with Musick's conclusion, what is your own position?

APPENDIX 5

The Call to be an Apprentice of Christ:
Spiritual Formation and Christian Leaders

Chris Hall, Ph. D.

Professor of Biblical and Theological Studies, Eastern University

Over the past 10 years I've worked with Christian leaders in a variety of settings concerning prominent issues in spiritual formation. Certain key struggles and concerns assert themselves as Christian leaders respond to the call to be deeply formed into the image of Christ. As you read the following statements, challenge yourself: "Is there an echo inside me saying, 'Yes, I have often felt exactly the same way! Those are the same struggles I've faced myself.'"

The Issue of Fatigue

"I must admit I'm tired — tired of running to so many meetings, trying to carry so many needs. I have been working so hard for so long that frankly, I'm numb. I haven't felt really close to God for months. Reading the Bible has gotten stale and dreary. I can't remember the last time the words leapt off the page as though it were a word of God directed right at me."

Some Christian leaders struggle because they are not very wise and refuse to affirm the goodness of the limits God has set for human behavior and endurance. They are not sleeping enough. They are overextending themselves for months and years in exhausting activity. A lack of balance and pace through the day is a recurring problem.

Discouraging habits

"Why can't I change? It feels like there has been no sense of significant change in my life for the past four or five years. I keep struggling with the same emotions and temptations, the same old arguments with my spouse, the same conflicts over ministry priorities and style with my board and team. It's not like it was when I was converted and everything was new and different. I don't think I'll ever change."

Leaders frequently struggle because they carry the burden of years of bad habits formed before they ever became followers of Christ. Some were abused as children and have painful, unhealed wounds that continue to fester within. Some simply have temperaments that are oversensitive or susceptible to depression or high levels of fear and anxiety.

The loss of intimacy with God and others.

"Even in large worship services I feel alone, dry, bored, even alienated. Things are not much better at home: I feel alone, dull, ineffective, drifting. My marriage is dead in the water. We have settled down to having the same problems, the same arguments, the same dead-ends for the last decade. I am almost always glad when I can leave on a ministry trip, and then I dread coming back home. Sometimes I wonder if I'm married to the right person."

Christian leaders often experience deep loneliness and isolation. They rarely have a small, accepting, affirming community of people with whom they can be totally candid. They deeply desire mature friends who will help mentor and model better patterns of living. Their sense of isolation increases when they fail to find places where struggles and longings can be expressed in confidential prayer and confession.

Disillusionment and the desire for authenticity.

"It's time to stop the presses and get rid of the public relations efforts of the evangelical movement. As far as I'm concerned we've oversold the spiritual life — made it shine so brightly in testimony and written books, in dozens of new techniques and secrets for Christian 'success in living' that the real humdrum of Christian living looks like a dead corpse in the morgue. I don't care whether it's the Pentecostals, the Deeper Life people, the Spirit-filled emphasis, a twelve-step spirituality — none of it works very well. We've got to get real, to be authentic, to stop kidding ourselves that there is a formula for success in spiritual growth and formation — and that you can obtain it by buying a book or attending a seminar."

And so forth: the four issues I've listed could easily be multiplied. They effectively illustrate, though, the conflict, disappointment, and disillusionment that almost all Christian leaders occasionally experience. And, at first glance, Christ himself declines to resolve these issues easily. Indeed, Jesus' teaching only appears to accentuate the inherent difficulties of growth into the image of the Son of God. For instance, Christ clearly calls his disciples or apprentices to change in specific areas — another list of four, but positive encouragements for growth and beneficial change by adopting a Willing Attitude:

Adopting a Willing Attitude—A willingness to leave certain things behind.

Effective Christian leaders understand and acknowledge the centrality of "leaving" as an integral aspect of spiritual formation.

"Leaving" entailed a radical change in vocation and livelihood for the first disciples. Peter, Andrew, James, and John were explicitly asked by Christ to leave their fishing nets behind and to follow him. The "leaving" inherent in becoming Christ's apprentice can also involve the loving and firm call to surrender deeply-loved or-loathed emotional, spiritual, or physical behavior patterns to the healing touch of Christ.

Many Christian leaders remain trapped by fear; if they are not in control of every aspect of their ministry, anxiety mounts. Other leaders are enslaved by ingrained patterns of behavior or attitude that have been consciously or unconsciously nurtured for years — for example, unresolved anger, ill temper, laziness, envy, greed, workaholism, or various sexual addictions. On a cognitive level, we understand Christ has called us to substantial freedom from these traits and behaviors, but we are unable to break free. The unfortunate result can be spiritual discouragement or deep self-deception. "Leaving" is an essential restorative response.

Adopting a Willing Attitude—A willingness to journey toward home with the perspective of a pilgrim.

It is notable that the earliest designation of the first generation of Christian believers is people of the "Way" (Acts 9:2). Members of the early Christian community practiced a specific manner of life, a "way," and viewed themselves as pilgrims on a "way," a journey. They had not arrived at their destination, but were continually moving toward home.

In addition, their disciplined manner of life empowered by the Spirit, a way of life patterned on Jesus' own life while on earth, enabled them to maintain the perspective of pilgrims rather than settlers. How should the image of believers as pilgrims on a journey influence our own perception of who we are as Christian leaders and what we are called to be? Would Christian leaders who view themselves as pilgrims moving toward home view their task, position, strengths, weaknesses, and struggles differently from those whose perspective is more like that of a settler?

The terrain of the land appears different to pilgrims than to settlers. That is, our present status as pilgrims can significantly clarify our perception of God's purposes and actions in forming us into Christ's image and sending us in mission to the world.

Adopting a Willing Attitude—A willingness to be taught.

Jesus often exhorted his audience to have "ears to hear" (Matt. 11:15, 13:9, 13:43). If listening well to Christ is a fundamental aspect of spiritual development, how well have we learned to listen as Christian leaders? How well do we listen, not only to Christ, but also to family, friends, acquaintances, and the suffering sounds of the broader world around us? How might the noise level in our lives prevent us from hearing what God desires to say to us? Have we become so busy, even in the good work of the kingdom, because we are afraid of what Jesus might say to us if we slowed down to listen?

Adopting a Willing Attitude—A willingness to obey.

At the core of Christian spirituality rests a basic question: "Who is in charge here?" For both beginners and veterans of the Christian life, this remains a question to be asked and answered on a regular basis.

Jesus insists on the centrality of obedience in his use of the imagery of the ox and the yoke in Matt. 11:29: "Take my yoke upon you and learn from me." The fundamental stance of both beginner and leader, then, is that of an ox or cow who submits willingly to a yoke for guidance. Why? Because of our inveterate tendency to wander in the wrong direction.

Our wandering nature has been aptly demonstrated in the lives of too many Christian leaders over the past two decades or so. We have become almost hardened to the news that yet another Christian leader has fallen into sexual or financial sin. The nature of the gap between the message powerfully preached and the hidden life of well-known pastors, evangelists, and missionaries has discouraged many Christians. In our more honest moments, though, most of us have experienced this same disjunction between what we know and how we live. In our minds we comprehend the gospel, but in action we struggle to practice its realities in our daily experience. The result is a gnawing sense of discouragement and unreality in our spiritual lives. Our words and lives are increasingly divorced from one another.

Are there pat, easy solutions to the inherent difficulties and pitfalls of spiritual formation? No. Would we want them if there were? Probably not. Perhaps the best path to follow in regaining a sense of direction and renewal is to head back to the beginning. If Christ were to spend the afternoon coaching you about your future relationship with him, and specifically how that relationship could be nurtured, what might he say? Might he not call us back to the basics of life as his disciple or apprentice?

The Call To Be an Apprentice

The issues, concerns, and practices of the spiritual life can best be learned and practiced at the feet of the greatest master of spiritual growth and development who ever walked this earth. To be specific, how did Jesus conduct his own spiritual life, day in and day out? What specific spiritual disciplines did Jesus consistently practice to cultivate his own relationship with his Father?

Take, for instance, the story of Jesus' active ministry recorded by Luke. Luke vividly describes how busy Jesus' life was: "Yet the news about him spread all the more, so that crowds of people came to hear him and to be healed of their sicknesses" (Luke 5:15).

Picture the scene as vividly as possible in your mind's eye. People in desperate need surround Jesus—people who are poor, sick, hungry, even dying. If Jesus had chosen to do so, he could have spent every minute of every day meeting the needs of the people he had come to save.

Yet observe carefully the next verse in Luke's account of Jesus' life. "But Jesus often withdrew to lonely places and prayed." Luke strategically juxtaposes Jesus' busy, demanding ministry (v. 15) with Christ's consistent practice of the disciplines of silence, solitude, and prayer. Jesus possessed a wonderful, internal freedom to step away from other people into solitude and prayer, so that when he was with people he would know what to do and how to do it.

If the incarnate Son of God developed a distinct coupling of intense ministry and specific retreats to solitude and prayer, how much more should we, in our much more troubled conditions? Jesus knew that if he exclusively ministered to others he would easily be exhausted by the responsibilities and needs that faced him every day. His frequent forays into silence, solitude, and prayer gave him eyes to see what he should or should not do as each day progressed. Perhaps more importantly, Christ's practice of silence, solitude, and prayer nurtured his life of intimate love with his Father, a love that in turn rippled out in Jesus' ministry to others.

The disciple of Christ is one who is called to leave certain things behind, called to learn to travel lightly as a pilgrim, called to listen, called to obey. Disciples can follow well only as they assume the stance of an apprentice, one who watches how Jesus lived, listens well to his teaching, and then chooses to imitate what the master has modeled.

The first step in spiritual renewal and development, therefore, is to immerse oneself in the life and teaching of Christ. Jesus himself invites us to dwell deeply on his life and word. "If you dwell in my word, you really are my apprentices. And you will know the truth, and the truth will liberate you" (John 8:31-32). Dallas Willard comments:

"If over a period of several days or weeks we were to read the Gospels through as many times as we can, consistent with sensible rest and relaxation, that alone would enable us to see Jesus with a clarity that can make the full transition into discipleship possible. We can count on him to meet us in that transition and not leave us to struggle with it on our own, for he is far more interested in it than we can ever be."

As a first step, you might consider reading the four gospels once a week for the next month. If this seems a bit much, try reading all four once a month for the next year. Immerse yourself in them. Watch Jesus carefully. Listen to Christ attentively. What is he doing? When does he pray? When does he worship? What is Jesus trying to teach us through his words and actions? What might he desire to say to us if only we would slow down long enough to listen?

Second, over the next year or two begin to immerse yourself in the history of the church's reflection on spiritual formation. Too often we limit our reading and reflection to modern sources. Dallas Willard encourages us to begin "seriously looking at the lives of others who truly have apprenticed themselves" to Christ. "Often his radiance in such people gives us very bright and strong impressions of his own greatness. To look closely at a Saint Francis, a John Wesley, a David Brainerd, an Albert Schweitzer, or one of his many well-known Teresas, for example, is to see something that elevates our vision and our hope toward Jesus himself." Who are the past masters of the spiritual life that might well offer the coaching I have needed for many years? Richard Foster and James Bryan Smith's *Devotional Classics* is a wonderful resource for those who desire to become more familiar with the riches of the church's history of reflection on spiritual formation, its inherent difficulties, and its promises and practices for renewal and growth.

Specific Advice from Expert Coaches

Christian voices from the past can help us move beyond specific spiritual roadblocks and occasional crises. The insights of St. John of the Cross (1542-1591) and Jeremy Taylor (1613-1667) help us overcome a common roadblock in spiritual formation—spiritual pride.

A principal danger in spiritual formation is the common tendency to divorce a disciplined spiritual life from the infinite grace of God. What will happen if we forget or overlook grace's central role in spiritual formation? Some of us will think that we are doing quite well...and fall into the crisis of self-inflation.

The crisis of self-inflation shows itself in several ways. The first is legalism. Legalism turns the disciplines into laws, and we end up basing our relationship to God on how well we are performing or progressing. From legalisms, we move into externalism and judgmentalism, attempting to judge others through the use of the laws we have created for ourselves. We become deeply concerned about who is measuring up and who isn't. A nasty spiritual competitiveness begins to infect our perspective. Pride erupts, resulting in the horror of self-righteousness and an exaggerated self-estimation.

St. John of the Cross speaks of self-righteousness and pride as particular temptations for those just beginning to practice the spiritual disciplines. "Beginners in the spiritual life are apt to become very diligent in their exercises. The great danger for them will be to become satisfied with their religious works and themselves. It is easy for them to develop a kind of secret pride, which is the first of the seven capital sins."

Spiritual pride, St. John teaches, manifests itself in a number of unpleasant ways:

- **A tendency to become "too spiritual."** People troubled by pride "like to speak of 'spiritual things' all the time."
- **Self-righteous condemnation of others.** "They become content with their growth. They would prefer to teach others rather than to be taught. They condemn others who are not as spiritual as they are. They are like the Pharisee who boasted in himself and despised the publican who was not as spiritual as he."

- **Prideful people desire to be noticed by others.** "...they begin to do these spiritual exercises to be esteemed by others. They want others to realize how spiritual they are."
- **People characterized by pride are often unwilling to be honest about shortcomings.** "They will also begin to fear confession to another for it would ruin their image. So they soften their sins when they make confession in order to make themselves appear less imperfect."

St. John of the Cross's remedies for pride included remembering that there is little we can do for God; thanking God for his gifts without broadcasting our giftedness to others; replacing pride with humility. "...they will focus on how great and how deserving God is and how little it is that they can do for him. The Spirit of God dwells in such persons, urging them to keep their treasures secretly within themselves."

Jeremy Taylor makes a similar point concerning pride:

"First, do not think of yourself because of any outward circumstance that happens to you. Although you may — because of the gifts that have been bestowed upon you — be better at something than someone else (as one horse runs faster than another), know that it is for the benefit of others, nor for yourself... Second, humility does not consist in criticizing yourself, or wearing ragged clothes, or walking around submissively wherever you go. Humility consists in a realistic opinion of yourself; namely, that you are an unworthy person."

Observe well Taylor's healthy and mature self-perspective. He holds together what we are apt to split apart. For example, Taylor reminds us that we are unworthy. God owes us nothing. It is not because of our essential worthiness that God sent his Son to die for our sins. Rather, Christ died for his enemies, those running from him at lightspeed in the opposite direction. Despite our unworthiness, though, Taylor warns against a feigned submissiveness or condemning self-criticism that only tends to elevate our faults and weaknesses.

Taylor offers a number of practical and potent antidotes for the poison of pride and self-righteousness:

- Do your good works "in secret."

    "Be content to go without praise, never being troubled when someone has slighted or undervalued you."

- Avoid "fishing for compliments."

    "Never say anything, directly or indirectly, that will provoke praise or elicit compliments from others... Do not ask others to identify your faults if your intent or purpose is to have others tell you of your good qualities. Some people will speak lowly of themselves in order to make others give an account of their goodness. They are merely fishing for compliments. Yet, they end up swallowing the hook, and they will swell up and burst by drinking the waters of vanity."

- Consciously practice praise rather than disparagement.

   "Take an active part in the praising of others, entertaining their good with delight. In no way should you give in to the desire to disparage them, or lessen their praise, or make any objection. You should never think that hearing the good report of another in any way lessens your worth."

- Avoid spiritual competition and comparison.

   "Never compare yourself with others unless it be to advance your impression of them and lower your impression of yourself."

- Identify compassionately with the weaknesses of others.

   "… look with great forgiveness upon the weaknesses of others. The truly humble person will try to see how the sinful deeds done by others were committed because the person was unenlightened or misled, concluding that if the person had the same benefits and helps that he had, they would not have committed any such evil, but rather, would have done much good."

Christ longs for us to draw near to him. He deeply desires to form us into his image. To be reshaped, however, we must assume the stance of an apprentice before his master. We must listen not only to Christ but to those who have followed him well through the church's history. Though Jesus might ask much of us, he promises that if we follow him as life-long learners, as diligent apprentices, we will find the purpose, fulfillment, blessing, and rest we have always desired.

For Reflection and Discussion

1) Review the cautions regarding spiritual formation from St. John of the Cross. Without naming names, describe two or three people whom you have known who have fallen prey to one or more of the issues John of the Cross warns against.

2) Hall summarizes Jesus' Call as four "willingnesses." Which of these do you find most difficult yourself? Which do you find the easiest to embrace? Why?

Family-Based Youth Ministry:
Fad or Focus?

David Olshine, Ph.D. Min.
Director of Youth Ministries, Columbia International University

SOME PROFILES OF YOUTH PASTORS:

William (Wolf is his nickname) is the youth pastor of a non-denominational church outside of Indianapolis, Indiana. His strengths are hanging out with his teens and training the adult volunteers. In recent months, Wolf has become aware of some angry parents who feel he's exclusive with only the "popular" kids and adults. Wolf isn't sure how to respond to this accusation.

Trevor has been busy preparing for his group's first mission trip to Mexico. Beginning in October, Trevor started publicizing the trip, and many of the students were getting excited, yet some of the parents stated they're against the trip, threatening to keep their kids from going to Mexico. These parents have no real knowledge of the trip, nor have they talked with Trevor. He is concerned that their dissension could lead to gossip and eventually the trip might be cancelled.

Trisha has been hired by a parachurch to work with middle schoolers. This organization typically relies heavily on adults to move the ministry forward, but as of late, there has been a drop-off of parental involvement. Trisha has never really been trained to work with parents; in fact, parents are the farthest thing from her mind. She was brought in to work with teenage girls. Why even bother with parents, anyway?

B.J. majored in youth ministry at a Christian college and loves the idea of working with families in the ministry. His program runs about 50 students with a lot of potential. One of B.J.'s missions is to involve parents at multiple levels. There is a big problem—the teens do not want parents around, and vice-versa. The kids gripe every time a parent shows up in the youth room. What options does B.J. have?

Anne and Rudy are the co-leaders of the high school youth group at a church that used to have a parent advisory team to help make all the decisions. When Anne and Rudy were brought on board, they noticed that during the youth meetings, the parents attend but do very little besides standing at the back of the room. If you were Anne and Rudy, how would you proceed?

FINDING THE PURPOSE

What do these five scenarios have in common? The answer comes first in the form of a question: What is the role of youth ministry with families? Mark DeVries's seminal book, *Family-Based Youth Ministry*, proposed that traditional models of working with teens without their families is ineffective. These true case studies deal with the issue of family and youth ministry.

When I began my youth ministry career, I was sent the message that teens were my primary focus. I was to counsel, listen, encourage, instruct young people. My title was "Minister to Youth"; some are identified as the "Youth Pastor." Parents and families were not part of the job description. "Don't mess with parents" was the mantra of the day. Some of us youth workers were actually scared of parents. Parents were even portrayed as "old" and "mean" at times; a phobia sometimes described as "parent-noia."

When I counseled a teenager, it took me a while to figure out that the parent(s) might actually be interconnected with a "problem child." Working with parents was just out of my orbit, and that of others.

Starting From Scratch

During my doctoral work, I studied a framework called family systems. Based on the studies of Dr. Murray Bowen, his data traced how family members interconnected. All families have problems, all homes have struggles—families are made up of people, and humans are complex. Bowen's research asserts that we are linked to our family systems from generation to generation, and with various problems such as depression, alcoholism, fear, abuse, and loneliness, these addictions can trigger other responses.

Bowen's thesis is that these "sins" can trickle down from family member to family member. As a fallen people, sin has passed from our forefathers to us and our children and their children's children. Problems, patterns, habits, and sin rear their ugly heads. As a young youth worker, I started getting overwhelmed at times with kids' hurts and pains. I would try to "fix them," only to send them home to their numerous family dysfunctions... and when they returned they were worse off than before! It took me a while to recognize that I needed some help.

I Need, I Need: New Needs

In the classic movie *What About Bob?* Bob (Bill Murray) follows his psychiatrist Leo Marvin (Richard Dreyfuss) on his vacation. When the two meet, Murray begs Dr. Marvin for some therapy: "I need, I need, I need, I need. Gimme, gimme, gimme." Murray is crying for help. Well, after a few years of youth ministry trench work, so was I. What did I need?

What I needed was a new paradigm. I was in need of "seeing" that the teenager was just one piece of a larger puzzle, one piece of the pie. The Hebrew concept of "family" is that all persons are connected: no one is an island. I needed a new vision, a new lens, a new way of thinking about youth ministry. We are all part of a family system. Attempting to help a teen without any connection to the family is missing a significant piece of God's plan. Placing a bandage on a terminal problem just doesn't work well.

What I needed was a new plan. As the Scriptures teach, the primary place of spiritual development and training is the family. As the home goes, so goes the culture. The family is where habits, patterns, personalities, and values are formed and cemented. As a youth worker, I must discover my role within the kids and families I am working with and develop a plan.

What I needed was a new partnering. At first, I saw parents as the enemy. What is a 25-year-old youth pastor like me to think when the CEO of a multi-million-dollar corporation mysteriously invites me to lunch, and his son (who doesn't like me) is in my youth group? With teens I felt secure, capable, and competent. Perhaps my self-perception reasoned, "You are seminary-trained and can help teens. You are called by Jesus to work with students." When it came down to considering ministering to parents and families, I was insecure, incapable, and incompetent! Again I thought to myself, "Olshine, you don't have a clue about parents and families, and until you start figuring out how to relate your ministry to families, your strength for the long haul will dissipate." I needed to change my thinking about how I did youth ministry if I wanted maximum and long-term effectiveness instead of short-term efforts.

Today I see myself not as surrogate parent of the teens I work with, nor do I see myself as their parent. I view myself developing a new way to partner with parents. I am more like an assistant, an advocate, not an adversary. I assist the parents to encourage them to be the spiritual visionaries and leaders of their children.

THEOLOGICAL BASE?

"Youth Ministry is nowhere in the Bible," one of my college students recently told me. I conceded in part, since "youth ministry" is a relatively recent (and Western) phenomenon. I also mentioned that worship bulletins, stained glass windows, and some of our contemporary religious symbols are not in the Bible either. "The Bible does speak about young men and women seeing visions and dreaming dreams; that God used young people like David, Josiah, and Joseph." I continued, "The Bible might not speak specifically to youth ministry, but it does affirm the role of the family in developing our relationships with God."

Raised in Judaism, I attended synagogue every Saturday (Sabbath) until my early teens. As Protestants can quote the Lord's Prayer and Catholics the rosary, Jewish kids from an early age can quote the "Shema" from Deuteronomy 6 4-9:

Attention, Israel! God, our God! God the one and only! Love God, your God, with your whole heart: love him with all that's in you, love him with all you've got! Write these commandments that I've given you today on your hearts. Get them inside of you and then get them inside your children. Talk about them wherever you are, sitting at home or walking in the street; talk about them from the time you get up in the morning to when you fall into bed at night. Tie them on your hands and foreheads as a reminder, inscribe them on the doorposts of your homes and on your city gates.

These words are directed to the family. This is not a job description for a youth worker! This is a family affair. The training is a process. The guiding of spiritual formation from parent to child is not an overnight miracle. It occurs over time. This is shepherding at its best, and the method is natural. The call to impart God's word to our children takes place at the most ordinary times: waking up, walking, talking, going to bed. These are informal methods of communication: no lecture stand, no podium, no Power Point! The message of Deuteronomy 6:4-9 to the church is that spiritual formation must begin and continue in the home; it instructs parents to share the things of God in a very natural way, not once a week but in a casual manner each day, "sitting at home or walking in the street; talk about them from the time you get up in the morning to when you fall into bed at night." In Jesus' day, the synagogue was always a supplemental means of "grace" to the home unit, never the primary institution for spiritual growth.

What's a youth ministry to do?

If the "ancient" model for ministry is through the family, then what does a 21st century model look like for the church? How do we help families who have "faith" and those who do not; families that are "messed up" and those that are unchurched? What about the rigid or families disengaged from the church and each other? How do we help homes in crisis? Do we only work with those who want to be "discipled," or do we spend all our time putting out fires?

Life is both vulnerable and difficult for parents. Humorist Rita Rudner once said, "My husband and I are either going to buy a dog or have a child. We can't decide whether to ruin our carpets or our lives."

Who will take care of the single-parent homes? How will we help kids and parents work through a messy divorce? What will we do to prepare our students for the "real" world when mom and dad are always gone? Are we more than spiritual babysitters to teenagers? Is family-based youth ministry a reality or a fad? If we are not to take responsibility for families, then what is our role? And so forth...

What does family-based ministry look like, really?

Context is king

Perhaps the most important questions are these: What do you want family ministry to look like? What do you want it to not look like? It will look different for a Young Life ministry and a mega-church downtown ministry. Rural and urban will be radically differentiated. Southern will look different from Northern. Developing a definition of family-based ministry be helpful, so here's mine:

A solid family-based youth ministry recognizes that the home is the primary unit for spiritual formation. The church comes alongside to pray, support, instruct, counsel, and help in any way that leads to wholeness in Christ. Youth ministry without a networking relationship to the families of our teens is no youth ministry at all. Working with the "teens only" model is not only poor stewardship; it is unbiblical. How will a ministry that is committed to youth and families be "whole" work in the contexts in which we live and work?

A Family Plan?

Using an acrostic of P.L.A.N., here are some beginning points for this particular journey.

> • **Program: Don't see family-based ministry as another program.** American churches start seeing everything as a program, and when that happens, they start piling the activities on. More activities tend to diminish relationships.

> • **Learn from Star Trek.** Captain Picard's word on the *Next Generation*: "To boldly go where no one has gone before" is a caption for us. If you have never been down the path of working with families, seek out some peers and mentors who have walked the trail. Don't try to go alone.

> • **Avail yourself of great resources.** Pick up *Family-Based Youth Ministry* by Mark DeVries; *Partnering with Parents in Youth Ministry* by Jim Burns and Mike DeVries; and *Tag-Team Youth Ministry* by Ron Habermas and David Olshine.

> • **Navigate slowly and steadily.** How to start? Begin slowly; don't bite off more than you can chew. I recommend anything from getting to know parents through an informal lunch to a one-time seminar in the fall. A small-size to large youth ministry (10-120 teens) can start with a "trial run," looking something like this:

> > **Fall:** Class for parents of teens for six weeks (Bible study on "Family Life" or "How to Talk with Your Kids about Sex, Love, and Dating")

> > **Winter:** Banquet to honor parents (teens serve the meal)

> > **Spring:** Parents' Night Out (provide babysitting)

> > **Summer:** Parent newsletter (informs them of events, trips, etc.)

Five Bad Ideas

> 1. **Doing nothing.** One of the worst ways of doing youth ministry is to leave out the parents. Ignoring families, pretending they are not there will come back to bite you. Are you living so large that you have no need for help driving the vans, cooking meals on retreats or serving on the missions trip? Are you going to leave out compassion when some families are "like sheep without a shepherd"?

2. **Doing something out of guilt.** Some youth ministries have heard the message of doing family-based ministry, but don't own the idea completely. So rather than figuring out why they are doing something, an event is plugged in out of guilt. This likely will be a flash-in-the-pan experience which won't carry much weight or impact!

3. **Overkilling with events.** In contrast to conducting a token parent meeting, some will hear this idea of including the family and swing the pendulum and do too much. I know of some ministries that schedule some sort of activity for families six times a month. That is overkill.

4. **Wearing you, your team, teens, and parents out.** A huge involvement with activities plus over-commitment to ministering to families will lead to burnout. The goal is completeness and wholeness in Christ, not wearing out your team, your parents, teens, and you!

5. **Being a know-it-all.** Most young leaders of students are unaware of the pressures of parenting a teenager. You might be an expert in adolescent development, know how to lead a retreat, speak at youth group, and guide a small group... but you probably don't know much about parenting adolescents yet. How could you? Unless you started in youth work later in life and have teens yourself, admit that you don't know all there is to know about other people's families, and that family-based youth ministry might be somewhat foreign to you. Once you realize you don't know much, your learning curve will grow off the charts.

Fifteen Great Ideas

These ideas are tried and tested. They start on the "easy" scale and finish with the more difficult ones.

1. Parent information meetings

A parent information meeting is to help the parents understand what is happening in the youth ministry—events, programs, trips, etc. This could be held once a year or once a quarter, depending on need; in homes, with great food and a casual atmosphere, or at your ministry facilities. Share your vision for ministry. Include time for questions and answers, allowing parents to voice any concerns. Have a handout with upcoming events, costs, and dates. Parents appreciate this kind of information. Keep the meeting brief and lighthearted (1 hour and 15 minutes at the max!). Why are you doing this event? Your purpose is simple: communicate, communicate, communicate. Believe it or not, if you do this one, you will gain instant credibility with your families.

2. Advisory committee

It happened to me a number of years ago. I actually stumbled on this idea when some volunteers on my team suggested that we involve parents more intentionally in our youth ministry. We asked parents that represented each grade of their students (sixth to twelfth graders) to be on a committee to help serve the youth ministry and to help us serve their families. Amazing stuff took place, from parents helping us develop a family-needs survey, to a greeters' ministry to welcome new people each week, a "dream team" that established resources, books, tapes and seminars. This committee could meet once a month, once a quarter or twice a year, depending on your needs. This is a place to ask hard questions and allow parents to talk meaningfully.

3. Nights off

I was feeling burned out one year in a big way. Our youth ministry had Sunday school every week; Sunday night small groups; Tuesday night outreach; retreats; service projects; and mission trips. We figured out that year we were busy more than 265 days of the year! That is ridiculous! I visited with some parents and they encouraged "nights off"... a suggestion that we followed quickly! Once every eight weeks, we called Sunday night an "off night"—no youth meetings, no volunteers' meetings, no training. We stayed home and let the teens hang out with the "folks." If teens didn't want to stay home, we had no jurisdiction over them—but we could insist that the youth building was locked! Our staff even provided a Bible study for parents with the kids over pizza. The night-off concept is model to teens and parents both: families need buffers for relaxation and reconnection. The idea also provides relief from the insanity of parents of middle schoolers always having to be chauffeurs. This off-night gives teens and parents a break. Chill out, okay?

4. Invite parents to youth group

Often, parents have no clue about what happens at youth meetings. Here is how to break the mystery: invite them to attend! Over a six-week span, I had my secretary call various parents and put out the welcome mat to visit youth group, specifying no responsibilities: just to observe and hang out. This helped everybody—it helped my teens get used to an intergenerational feel that "parents can be cool, too," and it helped the parents realize we occupied ourselves with more than just fun and games—the goals included transforming our youth into followers of Christ. Some of the parents liked it so much they joined our larger team. Some came back to share their stories; some were invited to teach on the team; some parents, just by being invited to youth group, became supporters and advocates of what we were doing (which helps at budget time!).

5. Home visitations

Visiting people in their homes is a lost art in need of rediscovery... and is reflective of a pastoral concern — "I care about you" — not a strategy of snooping up on them to see what life is "really like" for them. But you will discover that, for instance, just seeing the rooms of teens reveals what they like, value, and dislike! The families' turf is a place to meet them where they are; and the relationship you have with them will be deepened because of your visit.

6. Parent lunches (a.k.a. Undercover Counseling)

Everybody likes to eat, right? Set aside some budget money annually not just to take teens out, but to take out some of the parents. And here are the important items on the menu: let them know what a difference they are making in their kids' lives; ask them about their jobs, hobbies, and passions; get to know the parents relationally. Don't do all the talking; do all the listening! This is their time, and your chance to "counsel" by active listening. If you have a big budget, occasionally take out an entire family with the teens and siblings. Jesus shared meals with people; why not try it yourself?

7. Parent seminars and mini-series

The church is called to equip the people of God for works of service. What better way to equip parents than to offer an occasional series to help them be effective in their homes? Topics could be Communication; Spiritual Growth; How to Fight Fair; Boundaries and Curfews; Discipline; What is Going on in Youth Culture?; How to Monitor the Internet; Finances and Bounced Checks. These seminars could be over three hours on a Saturday morning, or a four- to six-week mini-series. These should be conducted by people whose areas of expertise are appropriate to the subjects. For example, "Understanding Your Teenager" is a seminar conducted by Wayne Rice and a team of youth communicators who have successfully charted their kids through adolescence (see www.uyt.com). Jim Burns of Youthbuilders (www.youthbuilders.com) offers a similar seminar about morals and spiritual growth. Or invite local speakers. I had a Christian psychologist lead a seminar on "teens in crisis," and utilized this as an outreach to unchurched people of our community, hosted in a neutral site. Invite parents of teens and pre-teens; you'd be surprised how many parents of third- to fifth-graders are already concerned and even scared about raising their kids effectively.

8. Intergenerational mentoring (discipleship)

One of the Jewish sages had a saying, "May you be covered in the dust of your rabbi." A younger man might approach an older rabbi, who studied and taught the Scriptures, and ask to be one of his followers. The custom was clear: if a follower of the rabbi were considered worthy to be a "disciple," the follower would literally walk in the steps of the rabbi, all day long. We have established that the home is the primary spiritual model for children's growth, but we must not abandon supplemental learning (schools, for instance, come alongside our families). The church needs to consider intergenerational mentoring, whether with small groups (one adult, five to eight teens) or one-on-one; or small groups with adults, and parents and teens, for mentoring. Jesus provided a model by calling 12 men to follow him; he lived with them for more than three years and taught them lessons of faith, trust, and how to work with people. So we can see that mentoring is not just a Bible study; it is helping people learn how to live. Paul encouraged Timothy and Titus to have older men guide the younger men and the older women lead the younger women. "Lone rangers" never make it; those who isolate themselves are more vulnerable to fall. Intergenerational mentoring is biblical.

9. Email helpers

Send out some email devotionals, cultural information, and other family-useful material that is available on the internet to teens and parents. One youth pastor has a monthly article and Bible study for his teens and parents that goes to more than 1,000 people in his church. Use email to encourage parents to continue the Deuteronomy 6 method!

10. Dudes' and dudettes' night out

A dudes' night out is like a father-son outing, and the dudettes' is a mother-daughter extravaganza. Do something active like broomball—rent out an ice rink, put on your tennis shoes and play hockey with sticks or brooms and an old volleyball. (The teens can "adopt" a dad for the evening—sometimes it could be a spiritual big brother or one of the adult volunteers in the youth ministry—if there are fatherless boys or separated dads gone AWOL.) Our girls have done, a "Night On the Town," too: broomball; dinner and a movie; or makeup tips and skin care makeovers. If you feel wild and out of control, try a father-daughter, mother-son date night.

11. Kids in divorced situations

As the epidemic of divorce continues to take its toll on families, the church must find creative ways to prepare teens and young adults for marriage, especially biblical teachings on sexuality, instruction about the importance of vows, and other pre-marital counseling.

We must also minister to those students and families who have experienced the breakdown of the marriage covenant. Consider pulling together students who come from, or are in the midst of, their parents breaking up. Let them talk, debrief, and process their issues. Some of the subjects that are pertinent are:
  - What forgiveness is and is not
  - How to handle resentment
  - What are some of the ways parents try to get their kids to align with one or the other's perspectives?
  - How to deal with step-parents
  - What to do with a bitter parent
  - Dealing with grief

Start with a meeting once a month, and see how it goes. This might lead to more counseling and times of processing. Kids in divorced situations need our support.

12. Long-range planning

This is one of the most difficult suggestions of this list, but necessary if you are going to take family ministry seriously. This involves coming up with an intentional, three- to five-year plan. Strategize where you want to be — not in a short-term, quick-fix way, but long-term. What will family ministry look like for your ministry over the long haul? Give it great thought and bring together a team of people to chart the course.

13. Parent retreat

Get your parents together for a 12-hour, or 24-hour, retreat. Provide resources and keep it fun and active. I have used outdoor initiatives (low and high ropes courses) to create a little tension, hard work, communication and unity building. Have some discussion goals for parents, addressing what kinds of parenting skills they employ. This is a hard assignment, but worth every moment.

14. Prayer teams

The Scriptures speak of the need to pray, the power of prayer, and ways to pray (Luke 18:1-8). Our youth ministries can develop a team approach, much like a "prayer chain" in which every family within our youth ministry gets prayed for often and regularly. Instruct your staff, parents, and teens to pray "without ceasing" for one another (1 Thessalonians 5:16-17). This sounds easy to organize, but it is not, so develop a strategy. It has been done by small groups, by geographical location, age groups (e.g., parents with sixth-graders pray for each other), by e-mail, or by phone. Involve as many parents who desire to pray as possible.

15. Parent-teen retreat/mission trip

This is not for the faint of heart! But pulling together teens and their parents is one of the most exciting events I have ever initiated, and I am grateful that I have risked organizing parent-teen retreats. One was a day-long event with the focus on "Listening and Communication Skills." Another was a two-day retreat on "Forgiveness and Conflict Resolution." Seeing parents and their kids hugging, crying, and praying together made God smile! I organized a parent-teen mission trip to Central America—parents and their kids working, painting houses, doing construction, praying, and evangelizing together (some for the very first time!) was awesome in its effects.

Closing Comments

Family ministry can be a fad, short-term and lacking in power, or you can ask God to design your youth ministry to be one of focus, ministering to families. As Jesus healed the paralytic man, he told him, "Take your stretcher and go home." May we be agents of healing (Shalom), as we assist as many homes as possible through the power of Jesus Christ.

For Reflection and Discussion:

1. Olshine states that "how kids are" can be understood better when we understand the family context, especially the parents. How have you seen this to be true?

2. In this appendix we are given four things to do (P.L.A.N.) and five things not to do. In each list, which is the most important to you and why?

A Hierarchy of Theological Responses to Popular Culture: "Knowing When to Fight, Knowing When to Embrace"

Chap Clark, Ph.D.

Associate Professor of Youth and Family Ministry, Fuller Theological Seminary

Many people talk about art and culture, but most people do not stop to consider what we mean when we use those terms. For leaders in Christian ministry, however, it is important not only to be able to understand what is meant by these common terms we all use, but we must also help people understand what God has to say about them. This article is offered to help those who serve God in leadership ministries: (1) to understand what we mean by "art" and "culture"; (2) to wrestle with what Scripture, church history, and tradition have to say as we seek to honor God in our response to culture; and (3) to be theologically prepared to assist others as they attempt to live as "aliens and strangers in the world" (1 Peter 2:11).

Defining the Landscape: "Art" and "Culture"

Although there is no clear consensus on the precise definition of culture, for the purposes of this article Clive Marsh summarizes a generally accepted one:

"Culture is a wholly human construct. In its most general sense it means the whole web of interpretive strategies by which human beings make sense of their experience. Culture is thus a complex field of enquiry, because it potentially includes all forms of human creativity, whether consciously meaning-making or not: art, music, TV, film, poetry, fiction, drama, sculpture, sport, religion, gambling."

This definition may not encompass everyone's idea of what culture is, but it does help us to have a working definition for responding to expressions of popular culture. It does this by allowing us to question our response as followers of Christ because it helps us to maintain a balance between our respect for culture and cultural expression ("human beings make sense of their experience"), and our willingness to address and even critique that which does not line up with God's intent for human activity and relationships ("culture is a wholly human construct").

Art, then, comes out of a given culture and is therefore intrinsically connected to the culture that has birthed it. According to Marsh and other cultural analysts, art and creative expression is a way a society (or any community or self-aligned group of people) attempts to make sense out of both their existence as a community and also the very nature of life itself. Some art may appear to reside on the "upper crust" of a culture (often described as "high" culture, like opera and period paintings) or on the fringe of a culture (as with more generally described art reflecting "pop culture," like "The Simpsons" or Shakira.)

Artistic expression may include a portrait that many in the society find offensive or a film that some find irreverent. According to our working definition any creative or artistic expression, regardless of content or following, is an expression that comes out of, defines, and even shapes the society from which it has arisen. Popular culture, then, represents a cycle of dialogue that any society looks to for the narratives needed to cohesively move that society forward.

Why Study Popular Art and Culture?

For anyone seeking to serve others in the name of Christ, it is vital that we carefully study and understand the popular culture and art that springs out of it. But the revealed essence of our Creator God invites us to live beyond that and to allow ourselves, along with everyone else, to be moved and even swept away by the depth and creativity of much of popular culture. So, if we are open to the wonder of God seeping through cultural expressions, we may approach popular culture from several angles. There are, then, at least five reasons we need to take the time and effort to be deliberate as we approach popular culture:

We are called to know those whom we are serving.

We are called to understand the world of those we are serving.

We are called to put into relationships and conversation our living faith in Christ as we engage the world and live as authentic members of a given society.

We are called to be a discerning people even as we live as aliens in the world.

We are invited to learn from and even enjoy the truth, beauty, and goodness of the cultural expressions of all people. As leaders, we carry the responsibility to help people think about how they live, and that means helping them to reflect on their lives and respond faithfully to the world around them.

The Church's Response to Popular Culture

More than 50 years ago, H. Richard Niebuhr laid the boundary lines for what it means to theologically engage with popular culture. Today, however, the default response for most self-described Christians to popular culture is limited to a single term of

Niebuhr's, "Christ against culture," where God is essentially at odds with culture and cultural expression. This view, relying on passages like I Peter 2:11-12 and others, often inspires a response to culture that "consistently critiques culture." In this mode of response, where we approach our dialogue with popular art and culture with the "outside and above" view that God is implicitly against what culture is and does, it is the responsibility of the thoughtful believer to find out how and where culture is "out to get us," and respond by blowing the whistle on whatever it is we discover.

But there are several responses to popular culture—some that are even friendly—that are both biblically congruent and theologically appropriate. The task of Christian leadership, then, is to help people to discern how God would have any given person or faith community respond to a specific aspect or expression of culture. The goal of this article is to provide the categories needed to facilitate that process.

Hierarchy of Responses to Popular Art and Culture

This biblically-grounded hierarchy describes our potential response starting from the (usually) least appropriate last resort and moving toward the most theologically desirable, or at least preferred.

This hierarchy is guided by the following assumptions: God has called us to love (Matthew 22:33ff.), and therefore all responses must be expressed with the motive of love, regardless of our appreciation or distaste for popular culture or any expression of it; and God has called us to treat others with "gentleness and respect" (I Peter 3:15) — that is, as we respond, we must be careful to treat others as precious, valuable, and worthy of God using them to teach any of us something about himself.

The hierarchy represents an implicit recommendation to attempt to respond progressively from the final option (see number six below) and work backward, seeking always to be a bridge-builder first and a distant critic last.

Hierarchy of Theological Responses

I. Attack.

"Be self-controlled and alert. Your enemy the devil prowls around like a roaring lion looking for someone to devour" (Peter 5:8-10).

Although this is often among the most common, or at least most advertised, response to popular art or culture, this response can be the most dangerous. The danger of losing our call to love, gentleness, and respect is difficult when we go on the offensive. There certainly are times when we must "attack" a particular idea or expression because the gospel or God's kingdom purposes are under assault. For this response to be adopted, however, we must have exhausted all other available responses first. If we are convinced that it is no longer an option to respond in any other way, we must remain committed to the truth that people are never our enemy.

2. Cheer and champion our heroes.

"Let your light shine before men, that they may see your good deeds and praise your Father in heaven" (Matthew 5:14-16).

When Christians attain notoriety or become popular, either as Christians or for their faith, then we will loudly and publicly applaud their success. An example is when a Christian recording artist "crosses over" into a secular market but maintains a commitment to singing songs of faith. We feel pride. When this person stops singing overtly "Christian" songs, however, many denounce the artist as "selling out." To stand with brothers and sisters who feel they are called to publicly proclaim faith through their art is obviously a good thing. But when it is our way to "show the world" we can compete with them on the public stage, we cut ourselves off from the rest of the culture. As this position represents a public display of a "we/they" mindset toward the society, and because our applause makes little or no impact on the societal landscape, the cultural wall created makes this a less than appropriate public response.

3. Hide or run away from culture.

"What harmony is there between Christ and Belial? What does a believer have in common with an unbeliever?" (2 Corinthians 6:15-18)

Although it is true that we need to be aware of those aspects of culture that can keep us from living as God has called us, the theological assumption often driving this response views culture as more powerful and pervasive than God himself. "You are the light of the world," Jesus tells us, and, as such, he never called us to run away from others to defend our faith in him, or to separate ourselves and create our own art and culture. This response, however, is certainly appropriate in our private decisions of life. We are not called to flee from culture, only to make smart decisions regarding the potential influence of culture.

4. Analyze and critique culture.

"Keep watch over yourselves and all the flock" (Acts 20:28ff.).

This is the most common response to culture in pastoral and academic settings, where as believers we are often viewed as being "brought out" of our own culture. This response is helpful in that from our temporal position of being "resident aliens" we must know and understand the culture in which we are living. This response is best used for internal training and dialogue, for once we publicly champion ourselves above and beyond our culture, the implicit arrogance of our stance stops conversation with the culture before it begins. This is one of the primary reasons why so few secularists allow themselves to engage in dialogue with believers; they sense our superior and disconnected starting point.

Upon analysis of the perspective of the above four responses to culture, each emanates from a "separate-from" and usually "better-than" mentality of the aloof alien. There are times when these responses are appropriate, especially as we attempt to try to internally discern who we are and what we are privately to be about in living in the midst of our culture. The following two responses, however, represent a more theologically appropriate external response to any cultural expression. It is when we recognize our common humanity with others in our culture and communicate that we all live under the same common grace of a God who cares, that our light will be more clearly seen and our presence will be more refreshing to a world that is desperate for light and love.

5. Employ for ministry purposes.

"Men of Athens! I see that in every way you are very religious. For as I walked around and looked carefully at your objects of worship, I even found an altar with this inscription: *to an unknown god*." (Acts 17:22ff.).

While this response has been popular in youth ministry circles for decades, the rest of the church is beginning to catch up to this highly effective way to connect the reality of life with the Gospel. To show a film clip, to refer to a neighborhood billboard, or to play a popular song is a way to help people realize that faith and the culture in which they live do intersect. This response is not an explicit reaction to culture. It is rather a *de facto* recognition that we are all part of a common culture and it is therefore a part of us, even as Christians.

6. Look for God's hand and participate as a fellow sojourner in the culture.

"Don't be deceived, my dear brothers. Every good and perfect gift is from above, coming down from the Father of the heavenly lights, who does not change like shifting shadows" (James 1:16-17).

For many Christians it is inconceivable that God could have any relationship to a "pagan" culture. Why? Evangelicals often look to the Fall but rarely to Creation to critique and deal with popular culture. Yet God is constantly in the business of revealing his love and purposes to those he loves. That God would care to use the medium of popular art, narrative, and culture to teach us all something about ourselves, believers and non-believers alike, lines up with his heart and his character of pursuing love as revealed in the Parable of the Good Shepherd (Luke 15).

Perhaps it is time for believers to first acknowledge that we are all part of the culture in which we live, and God has placed us there to be light and salt to those among whom we live. Maybe the day has come when a coffee shop has become a better venue for evangelism than the sanctuary, when a cup of coffee and a conversation about a movie two friends cried over will offer a better platform for witness than a sermon two friends sat through. Could it be that God is calling us all, believers and nonbelievers alike, to allow ourselves to hear God's whisper through a song, or a book, or even a beer commercial, and that as his ambassadors it is our calling to point others to the source of the Truth that stirs within the human soul?

May we all recognize that God does indeed speak in and through culture, in ways our theological categories rarely allow us to see, and that we can join with the Apostle Paul in helping people to see God in the every-day of human activity, art, and culture as he says, "Finally, brothers, whatever is true, whatever is noble, whatever is right, whatever is pure, whatever is lovely, whatever is admirable—if anything is excellent or praiseworthy—think about such things" (Philippians 4:8).

For Reflection and Discussion

1) Of the five levels Dr. Clark provides for a hierarchy of theological response, which one are you most personally comfortable with?

2) Picture this: you are a cabin counselor at a youth retreat and two of your kids have brought along some CDs which are famous for sexually explicit content as well as physical and verbal abuse. What will you do?

Bringing the Gospel to Youth Culture:
Working out Contextualization "with Fear and Trembling"

Duffy Robbins

Associate Professor, Eastern University

Take a minute to think about how you would respond to the following scenarios. They represent real-life situations faced by actual youth workers. As you read them over, watch for indications of the cultural phenomena discussed in Dr Hall's essay. Do you hear in these situations echoes of pop culture or postmodernism?

A youth worker plans a coffeehouse ministry. Should he allow secular music to be played in the coffeehouse?

A youth worker is planning a retreat and the kids on the design team for the event want to have a dance on Saturday night. Should she allow the dance?

A youth worker is speaking to teenagers in a weekly Bible study. He uses profanity to vividly make the point that sin is a really bad thing. Word gets back to the parents, and some of them complain about the coarse language. The youth worker says he was only trying to relate to the students in their own language. Was he right to do so?

A youth worker wants to use a scene from an MTV video to illustrate a truth in her Bible study. Some of the adults in the church are concerned that this might represent a tacit endorsement of MTV. Are their concerns valid? Should she do it anyway?

A youth worker is doing a session on the scriptural teaching regarding premarital sex. A student says that this is all well and good, but what if she chooses to be sexually active anyway—"not sleeping around with anything that moves, but maybe later on with my fiancé"? She wants to know if the youth worker is going to say anything about contraception. Is it appropriate for the youth worker to teach about various means of birth control?

A youth worker's ministry in an inner-city neighborhood finally seems to be making some inroads with those kids who have virtually no church contacts and no church experience. But she is troubled one Wednesday night when one of these very students strolls into the church drop-in center wearing a T-shirt with a message that is not only vulgar but insulting to women. How should she respond?

In one form or another, each of these case studies represents that place where an understanding of youth ministry overlaps with an understanding of culture. It is the place where classroom meets street corner, where theology meets sociology, where the Word becomes flesh.

Paul wrote in 1 Corinthians 2:1, "I resolved to know nothing while I was with you except Jesus Christ and him crucified..." And yet, over the course of the 14 chapters that follow (1 Corinthians 2-15), he writes about divisions in the church, unhealthy hero worship, sexual immorality, church discipline, incest, misguided tolerance, permissiveness, marriage, divorce, sexual relationships within marriage, food sacrificed to idols, causing the weaker brother to stumble, taking an offering, paying the preacher, temptation, the Lord's Table, drunkenness, male-female roles, spiritual gifts, authentic love, the gift of tongues, Jesus' resurrection, and life after death!

Why would Paul, who was determined to know nothing among the Corinthians but "Christ and him crucified..." take the time to address seemingly every issue under the sun except for the rising price of oxen and the latest prequel from the *Star Wars* scrolls?

Because Paul understood that this message of Christ and him crucified was a message with relevance that permeated every facet of culture and human life. Paul understood that the gospel isn't really good news unless it speaks to today's news, the good news and the bad news. Paul understood that we have a mandate to bring the gospel to everyday culture.

All Things to All People?

Massaging biblical truth into a body of real live people with complex problems can cause as much soreness as relief. But it can be done. Sociologist and theologian Harvie Conn recalls the story of missionary Don Richardson:

"Don Richardson relates in his book *Peace Child* how he ministered among the Sawi of Irian Jaya. He learned the language and finally, in one of their manhuts, began to share the gospel. There was almost total disinterest until he began to relate the story of Jesus' betrayal by Judas. Suddenly the men came alive with excitement. But their excitement and approval was over Judas, not Jesus. Richardson was dumbfounded. Then he realized that their understanding of the gospel was being affected by their worldview. In the Sawi culture, betrayal was regarded as one of the highest ethical virtues. Their worldview made Judas, not Jesus, the hero of the gospel. How could he share the gospel with them? Their worldview filtered the gospel until it was not the gospel. Richardson did not assault this value system; he began to look for a way of evangelizing that would use this cultural element with the least amount of disequilibrium. He found his answer with the Sawi concept of the 'peace child.'

He observed that a brutal war was stopped when a child of one of the two opposing tribes was surrendered to the other. The child would be brought up in the other tribe. As long as the child lived, there would be peace. Richardson now preached Jesus as God's Peace Child. To a world at war with God and itself Jesus was given by God as his Peace

Child. Only this peace was not temporary. Jesus was God's eternal Son, and God's peace was eternal. This was the beginning of the gospel breakthrough into that culture.

Richardson's ministry among the Sawi was effective in part because he was able to contextualize the gospel. Richardson was able to draw from his knowledge of the Sawi culture to find imagery he could incorporate to bring the gospel message alive for them.

We see this in our Lord's ministry. Jesus used contextualization when he spoke to farmers about sowing seeds and to sheep herders about being the good shepherd. Jesus used contextualization when he coupled miraculous acts with his "I am" statements in the gospel of John. When Jesus addresses the churches in the Book of Revelations, it is quite clear that he knows something about the culture of these cities. He is able to contextualize his message. He knows that Philadelphia is considered something of a gateway city for the central plateau of Asia Minor (see Revelation 3: 7-8). He knows that Laodicea is plagued by problems with its water supply and that its aqueducts (that channel water from hot springs) deliver water that is "neither hot nor cold" (see Revelation 3: 14-16). When Jesus issues to Peter—a fisherman—his call to service, he invites him to become a "fisher of men" (Luke 5:1-11). All of this is contextualization.

In his book, *The End of the World...As We Know It*, Chuck Smith, Jr. demonstrates in Paul's ministry a similar attention to contextualization. Especially helpful is the comparison he draws between Paul's preaching at a Jewish synagogue in Antioch (Acts 13:16-20) and his preaching at the city gates in the Asia Minor city of Lystra (Acts 14:15-17). Looking at the two messages side by side we can clearly see that he tailored his message to fit his audience, choosing to emphasize some facets of the gospel message with one group and other facets of the gospel message with the other group.

Acts 13:13-41 The Synagogue of Antioch a Jewish audience	Acts 14: 15-17 The Gates of Lystra a Gentile audience
How Paul addressed them: "Men of Israel" (13:16) "Brothers, children of Abraham, and you God-fearing Gentiles" (13:26)	How Paul addressed them: "Men..." (14:15)
How Paul referred to God: "The God of the people of Israel" (13:17)	How Paul referred to God: "The living God who made heaven and earth..." (14:15)
What Paul said about history: "God worked through Israel's history to produce the Messiah"	What Paul said about history: "God let all the nations go their own way" (14:16)
How Paul related to them: "My brothers" (13:38)	How Paul related to them: "We too are only men, human like you." (14:15)

What this chart demonstrates vividly is that our knowledge of youth culture can help us to know better which facets of the gospel message to emphasize when working with a particular group of students. The Willowbank Report grew out of an historic meeting of evangelical theologians and anthropologists from all over the world who gathered for six days in January of 1978 to think about the gospel and culture. The report makes precisely this point:

The Bible proclaims a gospel story in many forms. The gospel is like a multi-faceted diamond, with different aspects that appeal to different people in different cultures. It has depths we have not fathomed. It defies every attempt to reduce it to a neat formulation.

As Harvie Conn puts it, "If Christ is the answer, what are the real questions? Does God speak my language? How can we live out and share the gospel without domesticating the new wine?"

This was a challenge faced by Paul in his ministry to the early church. His letters provide several examples of thoughtful, faithful contextualization:

Acts 15:1-29. A conflict arose over two issues, both of which had to do with how Gentile believers who had readily accepted Christ should adapt to the standards of Jewish law. One question revolved around whether these new Gentile believers would have to be circumcised if they were to be truly saved. The other question, raised by Pharisees who had themselves come to be believers, was whether or not, after the Gentiles were saved, they should be required to be circumcised and obey the Mosaic codes of behavior.

1 Corinthians 8:1-10:22. This was the issue of whether it was permissible to eat food offered to idols.

1 Corinthians 5: 1-8. The situation in Corinth involved a man who was having an affair with his father's wife. Paul was not only concerned about this specific adulterous relationship, but he was also concerned about how the church was responding (or not responding) to the relationship.

Colossians 3:18-4:1. In this passage, Paul offers an exhortation to slaves to "...obey in all things your masters according to the flesh; not with eyeservice, as menpleasers; but in singleness of heart, fearing God..." (3:22).

The following table provides us a way of thinking through Paul's efforts to contextualize the gospel of Christ in each of these four scenarios. It also helps us to consider what it might look like for youth workers to be involved in this same important work.

Passage	Issues Involved	Contextualization Process	Principles at Stake
Acts 15:1-29	What is the method of salvation for the Gentiles? Do they need to be circumcised before they can be saved? And, if circumcision is not necessary before, what is necessary after they are saved before they can join in full table fellowship with the Jews?	The Council that convened around these questions declared (1) that Gentiles were not required to be circumcised or keep the Mosaic customs to be authentic Christians; (2) that Jewish Christians were not required to stop circumcising or obeying Mosaic customs; (3) that deference should be shown to Gentile Christians and that they should be offered full fellowship by Jewish Christians even if they did not adhere to Mosaic customs.	How do we discern what is cultural custom and what is biblical mandate? We mustn't require for salvation and full fellowship what God does not require even if it offends our cultural tastes. *The gospel demands that we make compromises for the sake of Christian fellowship.*
1 Corinthians 8:1-10:22	This was the issue of whether it was permissible to eat food offered to idols. The context is different from Acts 15 because within the context of the Corinthian church all the believers were Gentile Christians. There were no Jewish Christians whose feelings would need to be considered.	Paul communicates two pairs of truths: (1) this is not really about false gods, because these idolatrous gods don't actually exist (8:4) and no food is in itself good or bad. It's just food (8:8). (2) But, "the table of the Lord" is what the banquets of these false idols claim to be (10:16). Therefore, eating in the temples—at least in a place like Corinth—is tantamount to worshiping an idol. Thus, it must not be done. Okay, but what about eating that food outside of the pagan temple? That depends on the conscience of the individual Christian. Does it make you think of the idol? If so, don't do it. If it just makes you thankful to God for the food, then it may be eaten with a clear conscience.	*Meaning* is a key in determining whether or not a given behavior is appropriate for the Christian. *What does this behavior mean in a given culture?* If it communicates a non-Christian meaning, then the Christian should abstain. If its meaning is only objectionable in the view of some, then the Christian must abstain only in their presence. See 1 Corinthians 9:19-23. *Paul allows his ministry and message to be shaped by the lifestyle and ideology of those he hopes to win for Christ.*
1 Corinthians 5:1-8	The situation in Corinth involved a man who was having an affair with his father's wife. Paul was not only concerned about this specific adulterous relationship, but he was also concerned about how the church was responding (or not responding) to the relationship.	Paul does two things here: (1) He says, even your own pagan culture finds this an abomination, so that ought to tell you something; (2) Secondly, he says, even if the culture approved of this behavior, it would be forbidden because it goes against the law of God. There are two standards of appropriate behavior here. They are not equally valid, but they should both be considered.	The standards of contemporary culture are not useless for Christians. When they come into play, they should be considered. However, even more important than the standards of contemporary culture are the standards of God.
Colossians 3:18-4:1	In this passage, Paul offers an exhortation to slaves to "...obey in all things your masters according to the flesh; not with eyeservice, as menpleasers; but in singleness of heart, fearing God..." (Col. 3:22). This is a slightly different example of contextualization from the previous three, but it gives us a glimpse into Paul's attempt to speak to an issue of normal life in Greco-Roman society—slavery—that was completely foreign to his experience in Jewish society.	Paul is committed to addressing real life issues with the real live gospel of Christ. This can get messy. He speaks to where these people live without—at least at this point—trying to change the culture. While this may be disappointing to some, it needs to be underscored that Paul saw his as a very narrowly defined mission: taking the gospel to the Gentiles. Just because he wasn't doing everything doesn't mean he wasn't doing anything. It's a question of focus.	Paul does, however, plant some gospel seeds that could revolutionize the culture: (1) he reminds slaves and masters that their primary relationship is with God; (2) he reminds slaves and masters that they are equal before God; (3) he reminds slaves and masters of their obligation to do whatever they do to God's glory; (4) he reminds slaves and masters that, ultimately, both will have their work evaluated by God.

Passage	Cultural Question	Example from Youth Ministry
Acts 15:1-29	To what extent should the customs and norms of the believing community (churched people) impact the behavior of non-religious people who through belief in Jesus become a part of that community?	Church people are often offended by the behaviors of un-churched kids who show up at youth group—kids who don't know anything about norms of Christian behavior, let alone norms of church behavior. How do we help the church community to embrace these kids? What should be expected of these new Christian kids in terms of reciprocal behavior? To what extent should they be challenged as members of a larger family of faith to give consideration to their "churched" brothers and sisters?
1 Corinthians 8:1-10:22	To what extent might certain behaviors - acceptable in one culture - be unacceptable in another culture because of their meaning?	There are certain behaviors in youth culture that might - especially among non-believers - be typically associated with non-Christian behaviors: (1) types of dancing; (2) use of alcohol; (3) styles of dress; (4) profane speech; (5) types of humor; (6) certain types of music, etc. While there may or may not be anything intrinsically wrong with these behaviors, it is certainly wrong for a Christian to practice them if (a) it leads that Christian in any direction away from worship of God alone; (b) it causes a weaker brother to get confused about the faith.
1 Corinthians 5:1-8	Should the norms of the surrounding culture ever be considered in determining which behaviors are appropriate for Christians? To what extent should they be considered? What if "everybody's doing it"? What if "everybody's doing it" but God says "Don't do it"? How much can Christians heed the culture without the "salt" losing its savor?	There are a number of issues related to sexuality that fall into this category of contextualization: For example, there may be within Western culture a prevailing opinion that homosexuality is a personal, private issue, neither moral nor immoral. However, even within western adolescent culture, most teenagers find abhorrent the notion of homosexual pedophilia. Even teenagers who believe, "if it feels good, do it" would cringe at the thought of an incestuous relationship. Even most teenagers who feel that ending a child's life in the womb (abortion) is permissible as a matter of choice presumably would be outraged at the thought of letting the mother choose to end that life outside of the womb (infanticide). Sexuality is not the only instance in which we find such a cluster of issues. But, obviously, it is a critical area. Sometimes, as Paul did with the Corinthians, this line of thinking can help Christians to recognize that while they may feel their approval of immoral behaviors appears to demonstrate tolerance, it also demonstrates a lack of regard for the laws of God.
Colossians 3:18-4:1	How does one live out principles of equality and justice in an unjust fallen world? Does being treated unjustly give someone the right to respond with aggression? At what point does one claim one's "rights," and at what point does one exercise the freedom to give up one's rights? How does one live out the good news in a situation that is really bad news? Is trying to live well in an unjust, fallen system the same as showing passive approval of that system?	Teenagers are notorious for complaints that they are being treated unfairly—whether it's unfair parents, unreasonable teachers, disloyal friends, disrespectful adults, dishonest employers, or just bratty little brothers and sisters. Part of the gospel challenge is to help them think through what it means to be "free in Christ." These slaves were free in Christ, and yet Paul was calling them to be obedient to their masters. Yes, they have the "right" to be angry, resentful, hurt, disappointed. But, in Christ we have the freedom to give up our "rights" (Galatians 5:13-26). The gospel does not promise us that we will get what we deserve. Indeed, at the heart of the gospel is the good news that we will not get what we deserve. But, as God extends grace and mercy to us, we are called to extend it to others. This extension of God's grace came at the cost of Jesus' cross. We should not expect to pay any less in living out God's good news in a bad news world. Does that mean we are to be passive in responding to issues of injustice? No. But neither does it mean that we can treat with injustice those who have been unjust to us.

This article opened with some scenarios that any youth worker is likely to encounter out on the playing field of everyday youth ministry. Go back and take a quick look at them again. Are they really so different from some of the ministry questions that confronted the Apostle Paul as he sought to contextualize the gospel in the pagan culture of first-century ministry?

To what extent do issues of meaning and truth come into play when we wrestle with the question of whether we include in the Bible study on sexual abstinence some clear instruction about various devices of birth control? Or, when we debate whether to use a three-minute video clip with a powerful message from a movie that offers an additional two hours and 10 minutes with an awful message? When we limit our use of the symbols and stories of a pagan culture (whether they be in the format of music, or media, or just a kid's T-shirt) are we filtering out sin? Or are we filtering out sinners? Or is it something else altogether?

For Reflection and Discussion

1) Do what Dr. Robbins suggests in the second to last paragraph. Go back through the opening scenarios and link as many as you can to the ministry questions addressed by the Apostle Paul.

2) How would you respond to the question raised in the final paragraph?

APPENDIX 9

Common Ground—Multicultural Youth Ministry and Hip-Hop Culture: The Facts and the Challenge

Calenthia S. Dowdy
M.A., Associate Professor of Youth Culture, Eastern University

THE FACTS:

"Thank God for hip-hop!" That's probably not a phrase you'd hear in most evangelical Christian circles, but many youth workers have come to exclaim just that. With all of hip-hop's vices, there are certainly as many praises to make about this dynamic cultural revolution. Hip-hop culture evolved out of rap music, which is rooted in African storytelling and drumming. Africa's tribal poets, musicians, and oral historians were called griots, the original rappers. They rapped about what was going in the village. Young rappers today are doing much the same thing. They're talking about what's going on in their world and doing it through spoken-word art forms. Poetry slams, rap, vocalizing, and free styling are a few of the modes through which young people tell their stories. Hip-hop culture shapes "youth speak," their fashion, footgear, the preferred hair and dance styles, their way of life. It's more than just music; hip-hop is the culture of choice for many young people today.

The beauty of hip-hop culture is that it has bridged many divides. Hip-hop enthusiasts can be found in all ethnic groups and cultures. It stretches across social classes, from major metropolises to hidden rural regions; it leaps across every continent with its magnetic international appeal. Against this reality, rap music and hip-hop culture are not exclusive, special, or unique "problems" that urban American youth workers must learn to tolerate. Hip-hop represents young voices all around the global village. It is not just urban, not just black or brown, not just poor, and not just American. The face of hip-hop is also suburban, also white, also middle and upper class, also Asian, European, Israeli, and African. It is a multicultural, international phenomenon. And youth workers must learn to embrace the better aspects of it, realizing its tooling potential for reaching all kinds of kids with the gospel of Christ. Hip-hop is the common ground of today's global youth culture, and urbanism is the prop upon which hip-hop plays out its forms.

In his book, *A Theology as Big As the City*, Ray Bakke writes:

"By urbanism we mean the development of city as process—that is, the magnifier function of cities, spinning out urban values, products and lifestyles into a world linked by media, even in rural and small-town places. You see, there is no place to hide. The city is a media stage prop in this cybernetic era, and its presence will impact everyone eventually. So, even in places far from large cities, banks, businesses and families are linked up to urban centers."

Hip-hop culture links young people by way of the ongoing urban process, the media's global village. At the Coalition for Christian Outreach (CCO) Jubilee Africana 2002 conference, speaker Lakita Garth said it this way, "American culture drives the world culture, youth culture drives American culture, and urban hip-hop culture drives youth culture."

Efrem Smith, executive director of the Park Avenue Foundation for Youth and Family Development in Minneapolis, wrote in the May/June 2002 issue of *Youthworker*:

"Urban, hip-hop, and black youth culture often has an influence on the whole of youth culture—white teens far from the inner-city streets are influenced by the slang, fashion, and music of the 'hood. I've heard it said in many hip-hop articles that if white suburban teens stopped buying rap music, the industry would go out of business. If this is true, we must change the way we minister to young people. If this is true, we can no longer put up with divisions between urban youth ministry and so-called 'mainstream' youth ministry. If this is true, we need to question why most Christian music festival line-ups usually include 100 rock and alternative bands and three urban/hip-hop groups."

Smith brings up valid points for today's youth ministers to ponder. He goes on to say that the majority of today's young people are more urban than suburban (no matter where they live), more hip-hop than rock, more similar than different.

Popular rap star Marshall Mathers (Eminem) has a similar realization. While he has been banned by the FCC for indecent lyrics—and yes, his lyrics are arguably objectionable—his music has brought together diverse young people. Whether we enjoy it or not, he's a white rapper who has attracted an audience that crosses a wide ethnic and musical spectrum. He has even appealed to die-hard rock and roll fans. A June 2002 *Village Voice* music review reports that "Eminem's audience is no longer an expanded version of the hip-hop audience. It's bigger and whiter—a 'rock' audience." Rock, along with funk, rhythm and blues, gospel, and other genres, has been influenced by rap music's permeable abilities.

With these trends and sociological projections that say we're moving toward even greater diversity, ethnicity, and urban influence, conscientious youth workers must struggle to find relevant, common ground upon which to meet their multicultural harvest. The good news is that hip-hop culture has become that relevant common ground, a starting point from which youth workers can begin to reach out to their diverse communities. Hip-hop is like a bridge with solid crossover appeal. In a real, almost sardonic way hip-hop culture has had success doing what we say the gospel should do. It has bridged human divides and torn down walls of hostility. That's a kingdom mandate. "For he himself is our peace, who has made the two one and has destroyed the barrier, the dividing wall of hostility...Consequently, you are no longer foreigners and aliens, but fellow citizens with God's people and members of God's household, built on the foundation of the apostles and prophets, with Christ Jesus himself as the chief cornerstone" (Ephesians 2:14, 19-20). If only we could live out the gospel in ways that tear down walls instead of maintaining them. Christians can't boast of tearing down dividing walls of race, class, ethnicity, and nationality. Perhaps this is something we can learn from the hip-hop generation.

Hip-hop culture has united different kinds of young people under one common banner. Hip-hoppers agree on the essential tenets of the movement (MCing or rapping, DJing or mixing, breakdancing or poppin',' graffiti art, baggy fashions, and creative hairstyling) while at the same time celebrating their differences, unique talents, and other artistic contributions to the genre. They've managed to work out the "unity in diversity" idea.

The challenge

Efrem Smith said it well:

"Though kids today are being influenced by a black, hip-hop, multiethnic and urban world, they too often walk into homogenous youth groups that are led by leaders who, in general, don't seem to be paying attention to the coming multicultural youth revolution and the influence it's already having on their students."

It's time to wake up! The ways we envision and do youth ministry must be informed by this important cultural shift. Fear not, the core truth of the gospel message will remain the same, but the ways we reach out, shape, plan, and disciple this multi-ethnic hip-hop generation must speak with cultural relevance to their context. We must meet them where they are and share a genuine willingness to be there in their space with them.

I was still a teenager when rap music made its first commercial splash in inner cities. I was young enough to appreciate the new music and old enough to see and experience its evolution into a cultural form. Over the past 20 years I have ministered to and with young people in Philadelphia, Camden, N.J., and New York City. I worked primarily with poor kids in these areas, who were mostly black with numbers of Latinos and whites too. I instinctively used hip-hop's expressive forms to encourage them to share their thoughts, their pain, joys, and dreams. My greatest evangelistic experience was the night my Camden teen group put together a rap concert and invited kids from the community to attend. Jackpot! We packed the house out—brown, white, and black kids just kept pouring through the doors.

There were so many teens and pre-teens in attendance that the senior church ladies got nervous and went home early. I had asked them to bake cakes, pies, and cookies for the concert. I hadn't anticipated such a large crowd. Our teen think-tank encouraged kids to write and perform their own raps, which had to include a positive message. We provided drums, keyboard, microphones, beat boxes, tape recorders, and whatever else the performers needed. It was a loud, and some would say wild, Friday night, but we made new friends and cultivated new relationships. I met kids in the community I hadn't met before. I invited them to come out to small group during the week. Many came. My teen group was no longer ashamed to invite their friends to come to youth group with them.

Suddenly, we were a "cool church" because we embraced rap and invited kids to come share their talent. It wasn't just a program. Our goal was to build relationships by encouraging creative sharing. It was a time when many church leaders in the community were saying rap was of the devil and it shouldn't be in church. My youth group and I didn't believe the hype.

Youth ministry is a challenge. Multicultural youth ministry is an even greater challenge, but because of urbanism and hip-hop culture, the great divides are much more narrow than they've ever been before. Urbanism and hip-hop culture bring young people closer together and offer common ground from which youth ministers can begin their evangelistic strategies and relational programming. The current global village, with its overlapping urban values, postmodern paradigm shift, and invasive hip-hop culture, makes doing this work very exciting for many youth ministry professionals today. We're forced to think outside the box, making us more creative and more relationship-centered than ever before. In that vein, I offer five very basic and simple thoughts as you minister to young people of this generation.

1. Keep it real.

Young folks are smart and savvy. They can sniff out fear and fakes two miles away. Be as honest and up-front as possible. Don't be afraid of the difficult questions, issues, or discussions. Most kids want to go to the hard places and they want thorough answers, even if those answers might be more complex than they anticipated. I think this generation is more comfortable with the unknowable than we were. Not every question has a clear, simple, or pat answer.

"Now we see but a poor reflection; then we shall see face to face. Now I know in part: then I shall know fully, even as I am fully known." (I Corinthians 13:12)

2. Keep it personal.

Use the Bible to teach kids how to be disciples of Jesus, but realize that the best teaching will be what you model. You must model the life of Christ, not just preach it. This means that your young people will watch how you treat the other gender, your own mate, poor people, wealthy people, people of color, white people, homosexual people, and so on. More young people are dating and eventually marrying cross-culturally. How will you respond to kids dating outside their ethnicity in your youth group? It's cute to ask WWJD ("What would Jesus do?"), but the young people under your care see and experience you! They want to know what you will do. The want to know what you will say. This will inform what your young people will do and say. For better or worse, kids really do model the adults around them. "Be imitators of God, therefore, as dearly loved children and live a life of love just as Christ loved us and gave himself up for us as a fragrant offering and sacrifice to God" (Ephesians 5:1-2).

3. Keep it relational.

Evangelism, small group ministry, and discipleship work best when they are focused on relationships. Programs are only tools for building relationships. Kids in the city love to hang out on the stoop or on the corner. They enjoy talking, goofing off, and just being together. Don't discount this as time wasted. It's valuable relationship-building time. "Let us not give up meeting together, as some are in the habit of doing, but let us encourage one another..." (Hebrews 10:25)

4. Keep it creative.

Young people want and need to express themselves. This is why I believe rap music is so appealing. Encourage poetry slams, drama, music, dance, rap, painting, cartooning, graffiti art, T-shirt art, computer graphic arts, murals, even cooking and auto mechanics! Facilitate your young people experiencing God's spirit through the arts. Talk about God's love of creative expression. "God saw all he had created, and it was very good" (Genesis 1:31).

5. Keep it relevant.

Share Bible stories and lessons in ways that speak to the realities of your young people. Be sure that your materials have images that look like all your kids, not just some of them. Urban and multicultural study materials are available and easy to find. Kids must see themselves reflected in the Bible stories and materials. Get excited about the city landscapes of the Bible. Tell the urban Bible stories. Remind them that God is building a perfect city called New Jerusalem. All nationalities, tribes, and language groups will inhabit New Jerusalem. Cease talking about how evil the city is. Stop the impulse to constantly get your kids out, even if you think it's for all the right reasons. The city is their reality, and believe it or not, many of them love it. God is about redeeming the city. Your young people can be a part of that redeeming work. "God is not ashamed to be called their God, for he has prepared a city for them" (Hebrews 11:16). "Seek the peace and prosperity of the city to which I have carried you into exile. Pray to the Lord for it, because if it prospers, you too will prosper" (Jeremiah 29:7).

Thank God for hip-hop! Thank God for cities and urbanism. God has brought the world's young people right to us, all in one place. Now all we have to do is meet them there.

For Reflection and Discussion

1) React to the statement by Efrem Smith: "...the majority of today's young people are more urban than suburban (no matter where they live), more hip-hop than rock, more similar than different."

2) Have you experienced any good examples of youth ministry in a multiracial context? In what ways did this ministry demonstrate Dr. Dowdy's five ideas (keep it real, personal, relational, creative, and relevant)?

Jonathan Edwards, Religious Affections, and Spirituality in The Third Millennium

Duffy Robbins

Associate Professor, Eastern University

I watched the students at worship, several thousand of them, with hands raised, facial expressions that mirrored sincerity, and voices that coursed with intensity. It was a moment of wonder and mystery. And yet, as I stood to the side of the stage, preparing to speak, I couldn't help but wonder how all of this might be translated into the lives of these thousands of teenagers when the festival was over.

Would the hands now raised in worship ever get dirty by being raised in service? Would the students now so intent on "worship" remember that Paul characterizes spiritual worship as nothing less than presenting our bodies to Christ as a living sacrifice "holy and pleasing to God" (Romans 12:1)? Would those who stood up at late-night campfires to give testimony be willing on some late night in the future to stand up to temptation with as much boldness? Was this true spirituality, or was it just a really huge warm fuzzy experience of acting spiritual?

It was those same kinds of questions that troubled Jonathan Edwards (1703-1758), a young theologian and pastor in the mid-18th century, and led him to examine the very fine line between true and false spirituality. Although a thorough review of Edwards' study in true spirituality is beyond the scope of this book, his classic work, *Religious Affections*, is every bit as relevant and important in today's youth ministry climate as it was in the mid-1700s. It reminds us with unflinching boldness of the marks of authentic Christian spirituality. And while we are never in the position of knowing who and who is not truly spiritual, we may well be in a position as youth workers where we nurture and breed among our students a false spirituality.

Jonathan Edwards insisted that our religious experience is centered in what he called the "affections," described by Gerald McDermott as "strong inclinations of the soul that are manifested in thinking, feeling, and acting." Embedded deeper than either our thoughts or feelings, affections are the strongest motivations of the human self, ultimately determining everything the person is and does. What are these affections that offer "reliable signs of true spirituality"? Edwards identifies twelve.

A divine and supernatural source. True spirituality is the supernatural work of God's Holy Spirit in the life of a believer (see 1 Corinthians 3:16; 2 Corinthians 6:16; Galatians 2:20). It is not willful reformation; it is supernatural transformation, God at work doing in us what we cannot do for ourselves.

Attraction to God for who he is, and not just for what he does. The truest reward of loving God is God himself (cf. Matthew 5:46). As Edwards put it, "True saints have their minds, in the first place, inexpressibly pleased and delighted with the sweet ideas of the glorious and amiable nature of the things of God. And this is the spring of all their delights.....'tis the joy of their joy."

Seeing the beauty of holiness. In a culture that prefers to see God as not so great and humanity as not so bad ("I'm okay, you're okay"), true spirituality is a mind-set that sees God as infinitely high and holy and humankind as infinitely sinful and needy (cf. Isaiah 6, Revelation 4). But more than that, seeing the beauty of holiness entails developing a taste, an appetite for God's holiness. It's as if God gives us new spiritual tastebuds that allow us to sense as sweet that which the culture tastes as bitter and sour. More than anything else, for Edwards this is what separates true spirituality from false spirituality.

A new kind of knowing. Think here of the Hebrew word translated, "to know," used in Scripture sometimes as a euphemism for sexual intercourse (see Genesis 4:1). It points to a knowing that is much more than mere cognitive familiarity. This sign of true spirituality describes knowing God in a deep, experiential way (2 Corinthians 4:3-6).

A deep-seated conviction that the truths at the heart of the Christian faith are really true, a mind and heart convinced (Hebrews 11:1).

Humility (Psalm 51:17). This is not the same as self-loathing. It is seeing ourselves and others for who we really are. Edwards, in fact, warned against a false humility, very common in today's youth ministry climate, that offers humble confession of our failures without humble submission to God that he might lift us up out of our failures. It is a false humility that says, "I can't...," but then implies, "...and neither can God."

"They never denied themselves for Christ, but only sold one lust to feed another. [They] sold a beastly lust to pamper a devilish one, and so were never the better, but their latter end was worse than the beginning."

A change of nature (2 Corinthians 3:18). True spirituality will be accompanied (although not always visible right away) by an inner change. It will likely be gradual and ongoing, but as one old preacher put it, "This is not turning over a new leaf; it is turning over a new life." (See 2 Corinthians 5:17.)

A Christ-like spirit (Galatians 5:22-23).

Fear of God. Edwards' teachings on the fear of God recall a conversation in C. S. Lewis's *The Lion, the Witch and the Wardrobe*. The children, upon entering Narnia for the first time, are told about Aslan the Lion (the Christ-like character in the Chronicles of Narnia). The more the children hear about Aslan, the more they become alarmed.

"Is he a man?" asked Lucy.

"Aslan a man!" said Mr. Beaver sternly. "Certainly not. I tell you he is the King of the wood and the son of the great Emperor-Beyond-the-Sea. Don't you know who is the King of Beasts? Aslan is a lion—the Lion, the great Lion."

"Ooh!" said Susan, "I'd thought he was a man. Is he—quite safe? I shall feel rather nervous about meeting a lion."

"That you will, dearie, and no mistake," said Mrs. Beaver, "if there's anyone who can appear before Aslan without their knees knocking, they're either braver than most or else just silly."

"Then he isn't safe?" said Lucy.

"Safe?" said Mr. Beaver. "Don't you hear what Mrs. Beaver tells you? Who said anything about safe? 'Course he isn't safe. But he's good. He's the King, I tell you."

The current youth ministry culture is one in which our desire to portray God to students as "good" has often led us to portray him as "safe." Edwards would remind us that there is a sense in which our awareness of God's absolute otherness should shatter our frail self-confidences and delusions. And yet, as we grow to love him, the fear becomes less a fear that God will judge us, and more a fear that we will grieve him. Both are appropriate fears (Hebrews 10:26-31), but the greater is a fear that "trembles with joy" (Psalm 2:11).

Balance. True spirituality is marked by balance. For example, a balance of absolute assurance (Romans 8:39) with humble fear; the joy of forgiveness with deep mourning for sin; love for God with love for our fellow human beings; love for neighbor with love for family; public worship with secret prayer.

Hunger for God. True spirituality is marked by a desire to gain new spiritual ground in Christ (Matthew 5:6)—an ever increasing satisfaction with an ever increasing appetite.

Christian practice (surrender and perseverance). Edwards considered our commitment to a Christ-like lifestyle to be the "...chief of all the marks of grace, the sign of signs, and evidence of evidences, that which crowns and seals all other signs."

It is quite possible as we read through these "reliable signs of true spirituality" that we feel a growing sense of discomfort. Perhaps we feel this is impractical or unrealistic. It does not sound very much like the messy spirituality with which most of us are more familiar. But as we think about the process of spiritual formation and nurturing teenage disciples of Jesus Christ, shouldn't we also consider the question that Edwards poses to us from two hundred years away? What does Scripture teach us about true spirituality, and how are these affections played out through the combination of thinking, feeling, and doing?

Superfluous Journeys

Robert Falcon Scott, in preparing a report on his doomed 1912 expedition to the South Pole, two and a half months of misery that only led to a tragic end, wrote:

"I shall inevitably be asked for a word of mature judgment on the expedition of a kind that was impossible when we were all up close to it...Our expedition, running appalling risks, performing prodigies of superhuman endurance, achieving immortal renown, commemorated in august cathedral sermons and by public statues, yet reaching the Pole only to find our terrible journey superfluous, and leaving our best men dead on the ice..."

They must have been bitter words, and they poignantly describe the tragedy of an expedition that, despite misery and loss of life, did not fulfill its mission. But they are no more disturbing than Jonathan Edwards' words from two centuries ago that remind us that youth ministry, even when marked by heroic effort, inspiring words, and popular renown, is of little value if we merely lead students on a superfluous journey.

For Reflection and Discussion

1) Evaluate yourself on Edward's 12 signs of true spirituality. For each sign rate yourself on a 1 to 5 scale, with 5 as best.

2) Consider each of the 12 in turn. How can a youth ministry foster this happening in young people?